ALWAYS TOO SOON

Always Too Soon

VOICES OF SUPPORT FOR THOSE
WHO HAVE LOST BOTH PARENTS

ALLISON GILBERT
with CHRISTINA BAKER KLINE

SEAL PRESS

Also by Allison Gilbert: *Covering Catastrophe: Broadcast Journalists Report September 11*

"Pain" by Elsie Robinson appeared in the 1941 collection *Poems That Touch the Heart*, edited by A. L. Alexander. Original publication unknown.

Library of Congress Cataloging-in-Publication Data

Always too soon : voices of support for those who have lost both parents /
Allison Gilbert.
p. cm.
Includes bibliographical references and index.
ISBN-13: 978-1-58005-176-7 (alk. paper)
ISBN-10: 1-58005-176-6 (alk. paper)
1. Bereavement—Psychological aspects.
2. Parents—Death—Psychological aspects.
3. Adult children—Psychology.
4. Grief. I. Gilbert, Allison.

BF575.G7A55 2006
155.9'37—dc22

2006023884

Published by Seal Press
An Imprint of Avalon Publishing Group, Incorporated
1400 65th Street, Suite 250
AVALON
Emeryville, CA 94608

Printed in the United States of America by Worzalla
Distributed by Publishers Group West

Cover design by Gerilyn Attebery
Interior design by Megan Cooney
Photos © Angelo Cavelli / Getty Images

10 9 8 7 6 5 4 3 2 1

THIS BOOK IS DEDICATED TO MY PARENTS

LYNN TENDLER BIGNELL
and SIDNEY PHILIP GILBERT

YOUR WORDS AND ACTIONS CONTINUE
TO GUIDE AND INSPIRE ME.

I LOVE YOU.

***

*A portion of the proceeds from the sale of this
book will be donated to:*

The Ovarian Cancer Research Fund, Inc.
www.ocrf.org

and *The LUNGevity Foundation*
www.lungevity.org

TABLE of CONTENTS

FOREWORD
by Kenneth J. Doka, PhD

W HEN I FIRST BEGAN to offer grief counseling thirty-five years ago, I expected to see widows and bereaved parents. Certainly, I thought, the loss of a lifelong mate or the loss of a child might tax the coping capacities of survivors and lead them to seek support and guidance. I was surprised that a third of my clients turned out to be adult children who had a parent or both parents die.

In retrospect, I should not have been so shocked. The death of a parent, even in adulthood, can be a severe loss. For many adults, it is our first significant loss—the first time we ever experience that roller coaster of grief. If these losses occur in adulthood, they come when we are relating to our parents differently. We begin to see them not as the awesome or awful people of our childhood, but as people like ourselves—struggling, sometimes flawed—and often we have a new appreciation for their role. It can seem unfair to lose them just as we are appreciating them, understanding them, or even caring for them. When the loss occurs when the bereaved is a child, the death can, indeed, define our lives.

The loss of a parent may even sharpen our awareness of our own mortality. There is a great gap between understanding that people die and internalizing the statement "Someday I will die." As long as our parents are alive, we are buffered from the reality of death.

The death of a parent often creates a developmental push. When a parent dies, we may have to take on new responsibilities for the surviving parent, for other members of the family, or even for ourselves. When my father died, I realized that I would have to do the tedious work of reconciling my checkbook. He was a wizard with numbers, so whenever the checkbook did not balance, I would bring it to him. In both little and big things, we count on our parents. When one dies, we have to learn to count on ourselves.

When the second parent dies, things are even more complicated. *Adult orphan* seems like an oxymoron. In reality it is not. As long as parents are alive, no matter how old and successful we may be, we always know there is a place for us—with someone who has always cared. When our parents are gone, we are truly alone.

There are often other changes, as well. When both parents die, there is often a range of secondary losses. We may lose the family home. Holidays are different. Parents are often centering forces in the family—bringing the siblings together for birthdays and other occasions; now the axis is gone.

Sibling relationships may change in the wake. Parents may have been the glue that kept siblings together—the lid that kept tensions from spilling over. In some families, issues over inheritances expose

2

previous rifts, shattering a range of relationships and destroying the tenuous unity of the family.

This is why Allison Gilbert's book *Always Too Soon: Voices of Support for Those Who Have Lost Both Parents* is such a gift. There is value in the stories she has so carefully collected. First, they offer validation. Throughout the year, I speak all over North America about grief and loss. Most times I am lecturing to professionals about counseling individuals who are experiencing some aspect of loss. Often I do lectures for the general public. There the predominant question is a version of "Am I going crazy?" These questioners often recount normal experiences that we have as we grieve—perhaps that up-and-down sense as we ricochet from one emotion of grief to another, or maybe the time it is taking to heal. In any case, we often, especially in our first experiences with grief, seem taken aback by the process. Hearing the stories of others reassures us that our feelings are shared. It answers the question "Am I going crazy?" with the quiet reaffirmation "No, you are only grieving."

Second, these stories offer suggestions for coping. These can include areas such as how to manage family celebrations in the absence of someone we deeply loved, or more specific issues, such as who will sit in the chair that Dad normally sat in every Thanksgiving. As we read the pages ahead, we learn how others solved these same issues—large and small. This gives us ideas and thoughts that we can apply to our own struggles.

We do that, however, through the prism of our own self. Grief is a highly individual process, so the best way to absorb these stories is to ask ourselves how we can apply the experiences of others to our own life and circumstances. Their choices may help inform our choices.

The strengths of these subjects may also remind us of our strengths. Look at what helped them—faith, friends, family. What will help us as we cope with the deaths of our parents?

Finally, these stories offer us hope. However horrendous the loss, however difficult the journey, the contributors in this book persevered. Their struggles inspire us. More than that, they promise that even in the midst of grievous loss, we can, do, and will survive.

—KENNETH J. DOKA, PHD

Dr. Kenneth J. Doka is a professor of gerontology at the Graduate School of The College of New Rochelle and senior consultant to the Hospice Foundation of America. Dr. Doka's books include Living with Grief: Ethical Dilemmas at the End of Life; Living with Grief: Who We Are, How We Grieve; *and* Men Don't Cry, Women Do: Transcending Gender Stereotypes of Grief, *among many others. He has published more than sixty articles and book chapters. Dr. Doka is also editor of the professional grief journal* Omega *and the monthly newsletter* Journeys, *published by HFA.*

You may visit Dr. Kenneth J. Doka at www.drkendoka.com.

NOTE

a special note from grief counselor Lois F. Akner, CSW

IT WOULD BE SIMPLER if there were one way to experience grief. Then it would follow that there would be one way to get through it, one thing that would help us all. Alas, that is hardly the case. Grief is at once universal and unique. And as is evidenced by the stories in this book, we each experience it through a filter that is made up of our own history, the relationship with the person who died, the circumstances of the death, our resources—both internal and external–our beliefs, and our culture.

For more than two decades I have run a workshop, Losing a Parent Is Hard at Any Age, at the 92nd Street Y, a large cultural institution in New York City that serves the community, from babies to seniors and everyone in between. The workshop began when the Y took notice that there were not many places adult children could go to talk about this particular loss. Because the loss of a parent is virtually inevitable, people wrongly assume that it also means we are always prepared for it.

In the years I have been running these groups, I have learned that some people come through the doors wanting to speak; a few just want to listen. Most people want to hear from others, to feel less alone and to normalize what they are going through. It is through telling our stories that we acknowledge that something important happened and that we want help making sense of it.

In the first session of every workshop, I ask each person to tell his or her story. I bring a box of tissues. People sometimes knowingly laugh when I put them out; I am acknowledging that I am here for them, ready to listen, that it's okay to cry. It doesn't matter how many of these opening remarks I have heard; it is always interesting to hear what people emphasize, how they begin, what they include, what they choose to leave out. I'm convinced that the men and women in my groups remember and value these personal stories more than any theoretical concept I could offer.

Always Too Soon unfolds with such understanding and warmth that you can actually imagine sitting across the table from everyone who contributed. People talk about intense, private feelings, things they saved, what made a difference to them, what they learned about themselves as they grieved. It is enormously comforting to be able to nod in recognition of a feeling, reaction, fear, or concern. How helpful it is to someone whose mother died in her eighties to hear that someone else thought the loss was also too soon. We are curious about how others cope.

Take this book and treat it like a friend. Spend time with the people in it; you can read it in private, reread it, cry, remember, mourn, wrap yourself in your own memories triggered by something someone else has expressed. You will undoubtedly continue to find comfort in the lives, courage, and determination of the people you meet in this book long after you have put it down.

—LOIS F. AKNER, CSW

Lois F. Akner, CSW, is a psychotherapist specializing in family counseling. Since 1985, she has run a workshop called Losing a Parent Is Hard at Any Age at the 92nd Street Y in New York City. The author of How to Survive the Loss of a Parent: A Guide for Adults, *Akner has appeared as a grief expert on numerous radio and television shows, including* The Oprah Winfrey Show *and* Good Morning America. *Akner is a member of National Association of Social Workers; the New York State Society for Clinical Social Work, Inc.; and the Academy of Certified Social Workers.*

INTRODUCTION
by Allison Gilbert

MY FIRST PARENTLESS Thanksgiving came two months after my father died. My husband, eighteen-month-old son, and I went to my brother's to spend the weekend with his family. Despite the smile I wore, the celebration was doomed before it started. I was thirty-one, and both my parents were gone. I didn't feel old enough to be responsible for Thanksgiving. I was no longer somebody's child going home for the holidays. Overnight, I had become a parentless parent, feeling, as a young mother, solely responsible for my son's experience of Thanksgiving. I felt overwhelmed, and despite my husband's and brother's support, utterly alone.

I was also filled with self-centered anger. I felt a vicious jealousy of friends who talked openly about their plans for going to their parents' homes for Thanksgiving. I questioned why their parents were alive and mine were dead.

My parents left me while I was in process. I had just begun to evolve from single adult to married woman with children. My parents left me responsible for passing on family stories and traditions.

They left me without a direct link to my childhood. They left me with many questions unanswered.

They left me before I was old enough to be left.

***

My mom died from ovarian cancer when I was twenty-five. She knew and loved my then-fiancé, but died just before we were married. My sadness was so painful that I actually banned all mothers from my bridal changing room on my wedding day. Prohibiting my aunt and mother-in-law from entering was my way to keep from feeling the sting of my mother's absence. It was self-defense.

The final months of my mother's life, when she was the sickest and most frail, are now among my most treasured memories. I left my job as a writer and producer for a New York television station and moved home to live with her and my stepfather. There was no place now for the usual mother-daughter squabbles. My mother and I talked a lot. We remembered. I eagerly took on the responsibility of bathing her, ensuring that her IV flowed properly, and making sure the hospice nurse got a full report each morning. I played relaxing music, rubbed my mother's feet and hands with lavender oil, and made sure she felt adored. I wanted her to know how much I loved her.

Growing up, my mother and I did not have an easy relationship. My parents divorced when I was six, and when I was a teenager I was angry that the new man in her life, my stepfather, invaded our space and diverted her attention from me. Our fights left both my mother and me raw. Ultimately I accepted our new family dynamic, and my mother and I did more than just repair our damaged relationship: We became friends.

Ten years later, despite her weakening condition, our connection was even stronger. Now, as we were living under the same roof once again, the bond between us grew. She recited the recipes for my favorite childhood dishes, and I eagerly wrote them down. She shared a story about a necklace she had always worn when I was growing up; I never knew it was given to her by an old boyfriend. We sat on the couch, watched a "Best of Johnny Carson" video (her favorite comedian when I was a kid), and laughed out

Overnight, I had become a parentless parent.

loud. We even went on a road trip to Brooklyn and found her childhood home. I didn't know she was raised on Exeter Street in Manhattan Beach. Just eight weeks before she died, my mother threw me a wedding-size engagement party with a heated tent and elegant hors d'oeuvres. She encouraged me to invite anyone I pleased, and her guest list was equally extensive. My mother, who throughout my childhood had thrown much-anticipated holiday parties, held court. I didn't want to recognize then that she was essentially throwing herself a goodbye party.

My mom wanted to make sure she got to choose who received certain scarves and pieces of her jewelry after she died. No one was forgotten. My aunt, stepfather, brother, and I had an oddly fun time helping her; we laid everything out on her pool table, and the display spilled onto nearby tables and chairs. Each jewelry-and-scarf combination got a manila envelope, and we wrote the appropriate name of each recipient on the pouch. "My daughter-in-law, Randi," "My old college friend, Henri," "That nurse I liked so much." They were to be given out during shivah (the Jewish period of mourning immediately following death) and afterward. A little present, my mom had joked, for coming.

✳✳✳

My love for my father was magnified after my mother died. I held on tight to my final parent. It was always clear I was my father's daughter; we were both quick-tempered, stubborn redheads who possessed an inability to walk away from escalating conflicts. We had epic fights. Our most memorable fight happened in Moscow during the height of the Cold War—when our argument in the middle of Red Square attracted the attention of the police. They firmly escorted us back to our hotel. My father and I loved each other just as zealously; he was my unflinching champion, and I looked up to him more than anyone.

In June of 2001, my father and I went out to dinner to celebrate his sixty-third birthday. We ate Italian. I remember it clearly because it turned out to be our last wonderful meal together. He cleared his throat a lot during dinner, but it seemed like nothing to worry about. Then, in July, he and my stepmother came to visit me, my husband, and son at a house we rented on Fire Island, New York. He had trouble with the ten-minute walk from the dock to our home. He was short of breath. In September, just three days after September 11, my father died of lung cancer. He had not smoked in twenty years.

My brother and I didn't have as much time to prepare for his death as we did for our mother's. No one realized it was going to be so fast. I felt like I had whiplash. My father was treated, by coincidence, in the same hospital as my mother. It was a horrendous case of déjà vu. *Out of all the hospitals in New York.* The sense of familiarity with the corridors and cafeteria was not comforting, it was sickening.

The night before my father died in the hospital, a lung X-ray he was expecting was delayed and he was upset. He was tired and wanted to go to sleep, and he did not want to be disturbed by a technician. I was protective of my dad and made it my business to get that technician to my dad's room immediately. I hounded the nurses' desk, called Radiology myself, and had the department staff paged. I was ferocious in trying to make my dad comfortable. Ultimately, my tenacity paid off; my father was taken care of, I said goodnight and told him I loved him, and went home.

Before I went to sleep, the phone rang. My brother told me to come back to the hospital. My dad's breathing was getting more labored, and his doctors were considering putting him on a respirator. He had been tethered to oxygen tanks for weeks—with tubes up his nose and a mask worn over his nose and mouth. When I came into the room, my brother and stepmother were there, and my father was sleeping. It seemed that the urgency to put him on a respirator had passed, and the doctors were going to hold off doing anything. My brother left, and my stepmother and I went to sleep in chairs by my dad's bed. Hours later, I woke up and my dad was still sleeping. I began massaging his feet and hands because they felt cold.

Nurses came in and out—no one wanted to wake him up. Let him sleep, they said. The sun had come up. Doctors were beginning their rounds. He was still sleeping. Panic began to set in. We yelled to the nurses' station that he was not waking up. They told us he was dying. We called my brother back and summoned my uncle and my grandmother, my father's mother: "Come to the hospital, Grandma. Dad's dying."

Our family came and rallied around his bed. My father's oxygen mask was still on, and he was lying there peacefully, barely breathing. The nurse came in. I wailed, "Should the mask stay on or should we take it off?" I was thinking, *Would my dad want this oxygen mask on his face when he dies? If I take it off, will I deprive him of oxygen and make him die sooner? Would I be killing him?* The nurse assured me that at this point, the oxygen mask was doing nothing for him. As I slowly removed it, my hands were shaking. When I took the mask away, I could see that the elastic bands that wrapped around his ears to keep it in place had made deep indentations into his cheeks. His face looked so worn. He made quiet, breathy gasps for air. I got scared and tried to put the mask back over his mouth. Then I took it away again. I didn't know what to do. I was so upset that I left the room. My father died seconds later. At that instant, in that stark hospital corridor, the world was swirling uncontrollably around me—and I felt like I was about to be swallowed.

I knew that not even my brother, who had, of course, just lost his final parent too, could help me feel better. I'm emotional; he's cerebral. I need to talk about my feelings; he's fine keeping them to himself. I now acknowledge my parents' birthdays and the anniversaries of their deaths by lighting memorial candles; he doesn't pay attention to the calendar. While I have learned that

The world was swirling uncontrollably around me—and I felt like I was about to be swallowed.

reaching out to him on these special dates is usually unsatisfying, I feel compelled to call him anyway. I am always hoping I will get the connection I am seeking. Inevitably, I am disappointed. It's not that my brother didn't love my parents. It's not that we don't get along. It's just that he doesn't share what he's feeling—at least not with me. Nevertheless, he's my brother and I love him. I fiercely hold on to what remains of my immediate family. His very presence in my life brings me comfort.

Because my parents died of cancer at the relatively young ages of fifty-seven and sixty-three, they left me with the unnerving expectation that I will die young, too. I fear my children will lose their mother. I sometimes imagine my husband telling them that I died, and I imagine what life would be like for them without me. These thoughts have launched me into my own private war on cancer—a cancer I don't even have. I am by far the youngest woman at the radiology office when I get my annual mammogram and breast MRI. I am certain that when I go to the lab for the CA-125 cancer-marker blood test, I am the only thirty-six-year-old there who does not have a disease already. I have also sought genetic counseling to understand my risk. I decided that since developing cancer appears inevitable, I want to catch it early. I want to live.

Having lost both of my parents, I've become an expert on which belongings of your parents' to keep and which to discard. When my mother died, I kept everything. I wore her clothes for years in order to feel closer to her. I was twenty-five years old wearing the clothes of a fifty-seven-year-old woman. It must have looked bizarre. Later I was able to accept that these blouses, skirts, and jackets were never going to bring her back. I slowly allowed myself to give them away.

What I kept were her jewelry and her scarves. My mom wore vibrant silk scarves with nearly every one of her business suits. Because they were always worn around her neck, they absorbed her scent like a sponge. I remember inhaling them. Before I got married, I picked out more than a dozen I had kept and stitched them together into a large square. We attached the large swatch of fabric to four bamboo poles—and my husband and I got married under it. It was our chuppah (the Jewish wedding canopy).

When my father died, I did something similar with his ties. He had the best ties. I gave my favorite ones—the ones that reminded me the most of him and the places we had been together—to a quilter. The ties were cut into small pieces and used as fabric in a wall hanging. Still, I did not feel the same need to hang on to so many things after my dad passed away. His clothes were easy for me to donate; obviously, I was not going to wear them. (Although I would smile when my husband would wear one of my dad's dress shirts.) But more so because in the five years since my mom had died, I learned an invaluable lesson: Clothes just take up space, and I don't need physical objects to feel close to my parents. My parents exist in my heart, and I often hear their voices when I think. I learned that parting with their things was not a sign of disrespect, but of moving on. I feel liberated by not having the need to keep so much.

I still feel though, albeit less than before, that I lug around the shackles of grief. No matter how strong I feel, how accomplished I become, I want to share the milestones of my life with my parents. I still want their advice. Trying to put their absence out of my mind is nearly impossible. When I hear my husband talking on the phone with his parents—chatting about even the most ordinary events—I get resentful. A twinge of pain surfaces when I see grandparents pick up their grandchildren at my son's bus stop after school. So, I purposefully try not to forget my parents. Instead, I now incorporate them into my life.

For example, my mother loved nuts. She was a nutaholic. When my children dig into a can of walnuts in our house, I always say, "Grandma Lynn loved nuts." Or, when my kids play with their building blocks, I tell stories about how Grandpa Sidney was an architect and designed buildings too. It's a little something that I hope makes my parents more real. Sometimes when we celebrate their birthdays or a special holiday, I show my kids pictures of their grandparents at similar occasions and, in the case of my son's birthday, my father at my son's birth. I am convinced that showing them pictures this way means more to them than having the photos tucked away neatly in an album or in a frame on the wall.

It has taken considerable time and effort for me to put the loss of my parents into perspective. A few months after my father died, when I was hurting the most, I went to the bookstore to find a book that would help me process what I was feeling. I found nothing to which I could relate. There were books about losing your mom or losing your dad, but most books about losing both parents, it seemed, were written by clinicians. I wanted to read about how *real* people coped with this pain. I wanted a book to reassure me that I wasn't the only person so profoundly unsettled by the deaths of my parents.

So I set out to fill the void. As a journalist, I decided that the best way to plug this "book gap" was to find a diverse collection of people who have lost both parents and interview them. I started speaking with men, women, and children from all over the country who had lost their parents as children or as adults. I quickly discovered that I wasn't alone.

✳✳✳

Finding the right people to interview was my biggest challenge. There's not exactly a list of people whose parents have both died. In my search, I wanted to ensure that each person had a distinctive story to tell—and that when read in the context of a larger collection of stories, each narrative would follow a common thread, but not be redundant.

Not everyone wanted to speak with me—after all, this is a very personal topic. One internationally renowned author wrote me a lovely, personal note in response to my interview request. It read, in part: "Your project is a moving one—so moving that I find it impossible to contribute to it. The subject is always with me, and it is too deep for tears, and too private. I hope you'll understand."

Of those who did talk with me, some were young when their parents died; others were older. They are male and female, ethnically, socially, and geographically varied. Some have had experiences that you will relate to, while others' accounts are more unusual. The stories are heartfelt, candid, and deeply touching; they contain moments of insight, wisdom, irreverence, and in some cases, humor. And because all the interviews presented here are intimate, and address similar moments in dealing with this specific loss, I am hoping that this book will serve as a literary support group, providing guidance to anyone who reaches this milestone. As in any support group, some people have more to say than others. But each person presents a unique perspective. Taken together, their voices comprise a rich and varied exploration of this shared experience.

I purposefully began each interview by asking the same questions. The objective was to establish a baseline of information. *How old were you when your parents died? Did your parents die suddenly or over a long period of time? Which of your parents' belongings did you decide to keep and why? How do you keep the memory of your parents alive for your children? What was most helpful to you in getting through these losses? What specific ideas can you offer readers to cope as well?* (Please see the Appendix for a complete list of questions.)

Often, the conversations would go in other directions based on the circumstances of an individual's story. For many, the grieving process is made more difficult by the frustrated or conflicted relationships they had with their parents while their parents were alive. For others, their parents' deaths shifted their perspectives on their own mortality and their relationships with siblings, spouses, and especially their own children. There are similarities, however, to everyone's story. There is a pervasive sense of aloneness and an experience of grief not only over their mother and father, but for a childhood that is now forever lost.

For some, like author and motivational speaker Terrance Dean, losing parents brought out issues of abandonment. For others, such as writer Pamela Redmond Satran, there was a heightened fear of dying young. For Catheryne Ilkovic Morgan, whose parents were murdered in Auschwitz when she was fourteen, her parents' deaths kept her from having children of her own. She is now confronting the question of how to keep her parents' memories alive after she dies. And for Kate Carlson Furer, who fell in love with and married a Jewish man, the deaths of her parents thrust her into a religious vacuum; she is now solely responsible for her four-year-old daughter's understanding and celebration of Christmas and Easter.

For Sergeant Michael Treanor, Brian O'Hara, and Valerie Webb, some of the most horrific moments of the last several years—the Oklahoma City bombing, the crash of TWA flight 800, and the September 11 terrorist attacks—will forever be remembered as the very public events that took their parents' lives. Every time an image of these disasters is shown on television or an article is written, they must revisit the day their parents were taken from them. Learning to navigate the massive public outcry and the national tributes and memorials has been a unique challenge.

I also spoke with people we all *think* we know, including— among others—Rosanna Arquette, Yogi Berra, Geraldine Ferraro, Dennis Franz, and Ice-T. Press releases and celebrity biographies provide little insight into how these public figures have dealt with such personal tragedy. For many of them, this is the first time they have spoken openly about this extremely private experience. It is my hope that their stories will help you heal as well.

Loss, as many contributors affirm, can also be an opportunity to embrace change and reshape one's future. Thus, this book is more than a collection of heartbreaking stories—it provides inspirational tales of personal growth and spiritual rebirth. Singer

Rosanne Cash, daughter of music legend Johnny Cash, learned that "loss is a door to appreciation" and that "love survives loss." Her latest album, *Black Cadillac,* was born out of her own personal experience with grief after she lost both of her parents within two years of each other. Geraldine Ferraro, whose father died when she was eight, says she doesn't think she would have been as strong or resourceful if her father had lived. She speculates that he would have indulged her and that "I would not have become a prosecutor. I would not have been a congresswoman. I certainly never would have run for vice president of the United States." There was a similar revelation of strength for Rosanna Arquette, who, just days after her last parent died, was motivated to make a major change in her life. "It pushed me into changing my career," she says. Besides working as an actress, Ms. Arquette decided to become a director. These personal reflections offer lessons in how not to become stuck in the pain of loss, but to succeed beyond it.

My parents can still guide me—if I allow them to.

And you will. I have. In the five years since my father died, I have learned that being angry about my parents' not being around to give me guidance is a waste of time. All the advice I will ever need—as Mariel Hemingway so beautifully articulates in the first chapter—I received in the lessons they taught me as a child and young adult. My parents can still guide me—if I allow them to.

I've also learned to accept that my parents were not perfect. Time allows that to happen. My mother did not create a will until she was sitting in her living room attached to an IV pole. She was in denial until the last second. Her failure to assume responsibility created a probate nightmare that took our family years to settle. I refuse to do the same to my children. My husband and I have had our wills drawn up for years, and we update them often.

While most of the contributors interviewed for this book have moved beyond the immediate pain of their parents' deaths, most of us still experience pauses, slices of time when the pain is still acute. These surface when an event provokes a memory or a scent sparks a fond recollection. For me, coping today with the loss of my parents is like having a chronic low-grade fever: It is ever-present, but easily managed by a change of scenery or a good cry. Perhaps I should be happy with this persistent pain. If I didn't have it, as Dennis Franz reminds us on page 54, it would surely mean I didn't love them as much as I did.

No matter when you lose your parents, it is always too soon.

—ALLISON GILBERT

Mariel Hemingway

MARIEL HEMINGWAY
Time to Grow Up

WHEN YOUR PARENTS LEAVE, you're nobody's baby anymore. You have to take full responsibility for yourself. It is liberating and beautiful, and it takes you into a different phase of your life, but it's also very frightening. Suddenly you are an orphan.

Once my parents were gone, I realized it was time to grow up. A big part of me was still a little girl. Now, years later, I am glad to be in control of my career as an actress, the mother of two children, and take responsibility for my own business. I couldn't have done that before.

I MOURNED MY MOTHER FOR A LONG TIME

My mother first got cancer when I was eleven, and she was ill for the rest of her life. She had a malignant tumor attached to her thymus. She underwent chemotherapy and radiation at a time when chemo and radiation were horrific; the doctors couldn't pinpoint the cancer like they can now. Her cancer recurred and spread over the years, but the treatments were what caused most of her illness. Her immune system was shot, and radiation destroyed her lungs. She died of lung disease, not cancer, when I was twenty-eight and my daughter, Dree, was only eight months old.

Everyone in the family had expected my mother to die for years. The doctors had told her she had two months to live, and she kept hanging on. Many nights in my childhood, I cried myself to sleep, thinking that she was going to die. I mourned my mother for a long time. So when she finally died, it felt natural. I was glad that she was relieved of her pain.

I was crazy about my mother, growing up. When she became ill, I took it as my mission to heal her. At the age of eleven, I became her caretaker. I prayed for her, slept with her, took care of her in the middle of the night. I was desperately afraid she would die, and I thought it was my job to keep her alive.

My childhood was spent in Idaho, and when I was sixteen, after making the movie *Manhattan,* I decided I wanted to move to New York. The pressure of caring for my mother had been so difficult. I went back and forth between New York and Idaho over the years, to stay in touch, to make sure she was alright.

When your parents leave, you're nobody's baby anymore.

When I was twenty-two, I met the man I wanted to marry, and my mother was not happy. I had lived my life for her, and it distressed her when I fell in love. She was cold before and during the wedding. My parents didn't have a good relationship, and she gave me all kinds of negative messages: Your husband is going to go off and leave you; men are unreliable.

My mother was angry, but I knew she would get over it. She loved babies, and she later made a real connection with my daughter. Before she died, she told me I was a good mother and a good wife, and that my husband was okay and my daughter was beautiful. I think, in retrospect, that she was trying to make amends for our difficult relationship.

The day my mother died, I took a long walk. I ended up in a canyon, and sat down and tried to cry. I observed myself having no feelings. I thought, *Maybe I'm heartless,* because I loved my mother. But I remember somebody telling me that it takes two years to really mourn. Over the next few years, grief would hit me at odd times and odd moments. But I never became overwhelmed.

The time I really cried was when my sister, Margaux, died. I not only mourned her death, but my mother's too. I thought of how devastating it was for a mother to lose a daughter, which I felt powerfully because I had my two daughters by then. It didn't matter that my mother was already gone. It was still a wrenching thought and made all of my emotions, the ones that had been buried for so long, strikingly raw.

I wish my mother were part of my life now. I think she would have opened up as a person. My daughters ask, "Would she have liked us?" I think she would have. She would have continued to change, become more accepting, because of the connection to my girls.

THE PAIN JUST KEPT COMING

My father's death was very different from my mother's. He had gone into the hospital for triple bypass surgery. After the surgery, which was successful, he looked at me and said, "I know everyone is scared, but I am not worried about what's going to happen." I said, "Dad, you made it through the surgery. You're fine. What do you mean, 'what's *going* to happen'?" He said, "I just know it's going to be okay." All of a sudden something went horribly wrong. I went out in the hallway and screamed, "My father needs help!" When everyone came rushing in, I stayed in the room, and in the confusion no one noticed me. They cut open his gown and started opening up his chest. In that moment I felt my dad leave his body. I watched him, and I knew he was gone.

It was so huge; the idea of losing both parents was so enormous.

For three weeks he was on life support. When they did brain scans, there was nothing there. My stepmother was having a difficult time, but I told her, "You've got to let him go. He's already gone. I saw him go." Every day, twice a day, I whispered in his ear that I loved him and thought he was a really good father. I also said it was okay to let go, and we were going to be fine.

I brought my daughters to the hospital one day. I was ambivalent about whether they should see him—he was puffy and the drugs had made him look kind of weird—but I thought it was important for them to understand what was happening. When my maternal grandfather died, I was little, and no one told me what was

30

going on. I imagined that he just burned up in bed. It was frightening to me. And I saw the pain my father had lived with his whole life not knowing why his father had committed suicide. So it was good for my children to see their grandfather, to make a connection with his death, to have their questions answered.

When I said goodbye to my father, I cried a lot. Both of the girls came up behind me and held me, and that made me cry more. One of my daughters said, "It's okay, he's already gone to a good place."

After he died I mourned my whole family. The pain just kept coming. It was so huge; the idea of losing both parents was so enormous.

AN OPPORTUNITY FOR GROWTH

If you're young, losing your parents is crippling. If you're older and you feel crippled by the loss of your parents, you have to ask yourself why you allow yourself to be crippled by it and why you don't appreciate that it is natural and necessary for life to move on.

Sometimes we feel crippled because we didn't say things we thought we should have. I have learned that you need to forgive yourself for not doing what you thought you should have done. Your parents are not in a place of judgment. Their passing can be an opportunity for growth if you look honestly at yourself and try to figure out who you are.

After my father died, I developed the courage to be the person I am meant to be. He didn't hold me back; he was supportive, but I think I related to his fears. He was never able to be who he wanted to be. My father had always wanted to be a writer, and because of that, when he was alive, writing was something I couldn't do. It was hard for him—he was Ernest Hemingway's son.

I developed the courage to be the person I am meant to be.

I'm a generation removed, and I don't have anything to prove; I don't need to be a great writer. I write about yoga and my life. I am content when I am writing from a place of truth, from inside myself. I think that kind of fear is like a disease that you get genetically. When my father died, I was thirty-nine, and I finally realized there was nothing I couldn't do if I really wanted to.

I did a lot of writing when my mother died, and again when my dad died.

I often deal with pain through journal writing and poetry. Journaling is a powerful tool; it's intensely helpful. After writing for a while, you hit on something that's truthful about yourself, and you go on a journey to find out what you're feeling.

I REMEMBER MY PARENTS AT THE ODDEST MOMENTS

I treasure little moments I remember having with my parents. My mother did something when I was very young that I'll never forget. It was so simple. She let me rest my head on her chest when she was knitting or watching television. As my head went up and down, I could hear her heartbeat, hear her breathing. It was so important to me that I do it with my own children.

I remember my parents at the oddest moments. Whenever I'm outdoors I think of my dad, who was very connected with nature. In the outdoors he was purely himself. He made me appreciate nature. Often when I'm cooking, I think of my mother. She did everything from scratch. I inherited my mother's china, which she wanted me to have. It's very fancy; we use it for holidays. There was love behind those plates, and you can feel it. Holidays were when my parents got along best.

When my mother died, my father put all of her jewelry on the dining room table, and we were supposed to choose. There was only one thing I wanted—my mother's wedding band. It's just a skinny platinum band, but it has an inscription of the date of my parents' marriage. Someday I will give it to my girls. It is powerful and memorable for me.

The way I think about my parents' deaths is that they have risen to a different place. They're out of the pain of this lifetime. When I cry over them now, it's about the passing of time, about memory. Even though I lost my parents young and that was difficult, I know that they gave me what I needed for my lifetime. Everything they taught me, good and bad, was something I could use for my well-being and my parenting.

I don't think of myself as a little girl anymore.

Rosanne Cash

ROSANNE CASH
Love Survives Loss

I'VE LEARNED SOMETHING subtle about loss and love: Love survives loss. Relationships don't die; they just change. In some ways I'm closer to my parents now that they are gone. I sometimes get a feeling of being mothered; it just requires me letting go and relaxing into the moment. I'll be doing some real-world thing—like cooking—and suddenly I feel comforted. I'm infused with a sense of love from outside of myself. It's like my parents have gone to this realm that is pure love, and they're able to send it to me from that special place. I wish I could hold onto it for longer than I am able to. It's a sense of well-being—that everything is okay in the world.

With my dad, I've felt it plenty of times. Once, I got into a taxi and I could smell his aftershave. I felt a sense of being very present and feeling love in that moment. Or I'd walk into a store and hear my dad's music playing. That happens all the time, but sometimes it will be a particular song or line that's meaningful to me at that instant. Things happen to remind me that my parents are still around, that they care about me.

What I've also learned is that nothing is carved in stone. Some days I have tremendous faith that we're the ones who are asleep and my parents are awake—death is just a transition into a fuller life. Some days I have tremendous doubt—they're in the ground, and that's it, lights out. That feels very dark and empty to me.

My natural inclination and what I really believe is that my parents exist intact somewhere in another realm that I'm just too dense to experience. And that is what I'd like to pass on to my children. I don't want them to feel an empty, dark despair that there's nothingness afterward. I started thinking, *Could I ever leave my children?*

No, not even in death.

So have my parents left me? No, they haven't.

IT REQUIRED DISCIPLINE TO GRIEVE PRIVATELY FOR MY FATHER

My father died in 2003, when I was forty-eight. The official cause of death was complications of diabetes, but he also had autonomic neuropathy, damage to his nerves. His death was a moment that I'll never forget, that I always carry with me—a point in time that felt like great peace, full of light in the room.

The day after my dad died, all four of my daughters came and got into bed with me. I could see them putting their own feelings aside to help me, and I was so proud of them. My husband was also amazing. He put his own needs aside for a year; he was so patient. I could not have given my husband what he gave to me.

One element of losing my dad was that I had to be meticulous about separating myself from public expressions of grief and not getting sucked into an attempt to turn him into an icon. The public kind of appropriated a lot of the grief of losing my dad. You can't imagine the hundreds of things I got in the mail—songs written for him, plays written for him, paintings made for him, screenplays, books, memorial concerts, television shows. It was endless. As soon as I read the first sentence of an unsolicited piece of mail, I'd throw it out—I just couldn't deal with it. It was intrusive stuff, like, "Here's a song I wrote about your dad, and I'd really love for you to sing it. You're the only one who can pack the emotional wallop." They were trying to use my feelings.

In some ways, I'm closer to my parents now that they are gone.

However, the letters—the personal expressions of love and sympathy from his fans—were what I really valued. I saved many of them; they were so kind. Particularly people who had lost their parents and who gave me encouragement and hope. Total strangers took the time to do that, and I thought that was beautiful.

It required discipline to grieve privately for my father.

I couldn't go to the gym without looking up at the TV screen in front of the treadmill and seeing yet another show about my dad. I knew there was going to be a public expression of grief for him, and I thought I was prepared for it. But I wasn't. When I went out in public, people who recognized me came up, wanting to grieve with me about the loss of my own father. I sometimes found this to be incredibly insensitive, to tell you the truth.

I didn't pick up magazines, and I stopped turning on the TV. For the first year after my dad died, every time I saw a picture of him, it had dates underneath his name. My husband said, "Nobody should have to see their parent's picture bracketed by the dates of their birth and death." You should be able to prepare yourself to see that—like when you go to the cemetery. Because it's shocking. We were constantly bombarded. Even now the movie *Walk the Line* and the Broadway show *Ring of Fire* are just too much. Perhaps if they were done ten years from now, I'd feel differently.

On the anniversary of his death, I arranged a private memorial service. There had been so many public ones. It was invitation only, at my church, St. Luke's Episcopal Church in Greenwich Village.

BECOMING THE MATRIARCH OF THE FAMILY

My mother died in 2005, on my fiftieth birthday. She had lung cancer, but she actually died of an infection following surgery. Everybody was with her at the hospital—all of her kids, her husband, her grandchildren, her sister, her nephew. There were about twenty people in the room. It was how she wanted it. We sat with her body for an hour after she passed away. It was incredibly precious time. I'm so happy we did that. Even though we're not Jewish, my sister and I decided to sit shivah (the Jewish period of mourning immediately following death).

The day after my mother died, my sister said something amazing to me. I think she was trying to make me feel better, and she said, "Mom gave you the gift of becoming the matriarch of the family on your birthday." I've held onto that thought. I'm the oldest daughter—and I can step into that role. That's been empowering. I have always felt a certain responsibility to keep the family together, keep communications open. I'm kind of bossy, and I like to be in control. So it comes naturally to me.

Having experienced the death of my father, I didn't have that gut-wrenching shock when my mother died because I knew I could survive the death. I was stronger. But that didn't make the intensity of the grief any less. Since my parents died so close together, it was like a one-two punch. I was walking into walls for the first six months after my mom's death. But my mother's death didn't require the same emotional discipline that my father's had. She was a very private person, so I was able to grieve for my mother with more ease than I was able to with my father.

Relationships founded on love don't end when one person leaves the planet.

I'm looking forward to getting past the first anniversary of my mother's death. Everybody said, "It'll take a year" when my father died. I didn't know what they were talking about until I got through that first year. The weight lifted a bit after the first anniversary of my dad's death, and I said, "Oh, I get it." It takes a year because you have to go through every first holiday and birthday without them, and then the first anniversary of their death. Once that's done, you feel like you've completed the most intense part of the cycle.

A DOOR TO APPRECIATION

In a two-year period, I lost not only my parents but my stepmother, my stepsister, my aunt, and my godfather. There was a tidal wave of loss. There are moments I definitely still feel like an orphan.

Because I'm an artist, I took those feelings to work. What felt unmanageable became manageable. Applying a sense of poetry and my discipline as a writer to those overwhelming feelings was tremendously useful to me. My concern in doing my latest album, though, was that I might lose my focus as a writer and become self-indulgent or sentimental. That would have been a kind of artistic death.

The songs on my new record, *Black Cadillac,* are all about different facets of loss. There are feelings of anger, denial, doubt—everything that goes along with grief, even transcendence. There is also an understanding that loss is a door to appreciation and that relationships founded on love don't end when one person leaves the planet.

This whole experience has made me a stronger mother.

So in that way, my album is universal; my experience of grief is similar to how we *all* experience grief. There's no cheating it, and there's no way around it. You can only go through it. I recognize, too, that the album is archival. There are a lot of documentary details in there about my own life. I realized, a few months after finishing the record, that I had actually made it for my kids. It is a road map for them for the future, when they lose me.

I have been writing and recording songs for almost thirty years now, and while I have worked hard to achieve success on my own, I find it frustrating that my work continues to be evaluated in the context of my father's, as if I'm an accessory to him. That's something I've been dealing with my whole life. Interviewers want to talk about the backstory, but the backstory is not what my record is about. It's not fair to pillage my private life, rummage through my deepest feelings, use it as fodder for an interview. Then they go off and write a story, while I go home and have to deal with those feelings for the rest of the day.

THE LETTER

In the privacy of my own home, I grieve and remember, like everyone else.

I have my father's private desk that he used every day in his little office. He taped the edges with gauze because he kept banging the sharp corners into his knees; diabetics have to be careful of their skin. So I kept the gauze on the corners. I love that desk; to me, it just signifies him. A lot of creative work went on there.

My father's house was just sold. It was very painful to lose a childhood home. In fact, we lost two homes, because we had to sell his house in Jamaica and the house in Tennessee. They're huge and expensive; none of us could have afforded to keep them. My father lived in a different financial stratum from the rest of us. There's a tremendous feeling of loss around that. I've come to accept, though, that the love and the memories that happened there remain.

For some time after my father's death, I couldn't listen to his music. Now it gives me comfort. I use the music in a personal way. I played *Ballads of the True West* for my seven-year-old son, who never heard it, and said, "Listen to this great song." Now he's really into it—it's a way to keep him connected with his grandpa.

My mother crocheted, so I have her crocheted blankets. They mean everything to me. She also wrote prayers to me and kept them in a special box. There are dozens. She never shared them with me when she was alive; we only found them later. I love those prayers.

This whole experience has made me a stronger mother. I'm fiercer in my connection to my children. I plan to leave them my diaries, letters, and jewelry. I have written letters to them, documenting certain things about their lives now. I haven't told them yet. I probably will as I get older. Or maybe not—maybe they can just find them.

I wish that my parents had left me more. I wish that there were a sealed letter somewhere that said, "To Rosanne," and that I found it. But it's not in either of their natures to do that. And I understand that.

But I did discover a letter buried in my father's papers that I found truly transformative. It wasn't written to me; he had written it to a friend who had just lost his father. It was as if he kept a copy so my three sisters and my brother would find it. When I read the letter, it was as if he were speaking to me. It was a gift. In it he said, "You are now free to assume the best qualities of your parent. And in that way he will live on."

I took this really seriously. I started thinking, *What are the best qualities of my parents that I would like to assimilate into myself—that I would like to let live through me? Their integrity? Their loyalty?*

To integrate those things into my own personality, I find, is the best way to keep them living.

Dennis Franz

DENNIS FRANZ
I'm Glad that I Miss Them

YOU ONLY GET one set of parents. If you're close to them at all, you know how important it is to lose the biggest influence on your life. It takes a long time to adjust to the fact that you can't give your parents a call or go home for the holidays to see them. You won't get letters from them, send and receive gifts, or talk to them. You realize that part of the joy of success, of good things happening in your life, is sharing them. When you can't share your happiness with your parents, it reminds you how much you miss them. And how much you loved them.

THE SAME HOSPITAL AT THE SAME TIME

My dad was a very private man, so when the doctor took out a tumor in my dad's colon and told us that it was too late, that it had already spread, we decided to wait until Dad talked to us rather than bring it up. He underwent some chemo treatments; he thought he was going to improve. We were kind of living with false hope. He only lived for about six months after the diagnosis.

Dad had always been a strong, virile guy. Now he was getting smaller and frail. He had no energy and was in a lot of pain. It was hard to watch him deteriorating, becoming weaker and less vibrant. Emotionally, I think he understood what was happening, but he never talked about death, about the end, or about succumbing to the cancer. It was never discussed. We just tried to be optimistic in the face of complete adversity and make him feel as good as possible.

During that time, which was stressful for all of us, my mom woke up one morning with dad and said, "I feel dizzy, lightheaded. Do I look funny? Am I talking funny?" And then she collapsed. She had a stroke and went into the hospital. My parents were in the same hospital at the same time. As time went on, my dad got worse, and my mother was in a coma. I felt like I was at a tennis match, going from one room to the other.

Then Dad got so bad that he had to be taken out of the hospital. Hospice came to my parents' home.

When my parents died I was working. I may have been selfishly taking my intense focus off that situation and putting it on my work. I was more able to take my mind off my parents' dying than my sisters, who were there all the time. I was on the phone with my sister when my dad died. She had been saying that he wasn't responding well, and today was not a good day. All of a sudden the conversation was broken. She said, "Oh, wait a minute—hold on. Oh!" Then she said, "Dad's gone." He was seventy-four.

Our mother was in a coma for several weeks after our father died. She was kept alive by a machine. The doctors encouraged us to pull the plug; they said that she'd been too long in that state and it would be wiser and more humane to let her go. We asked whether there was any hope, and they said, "Of course, there are always miracles and there's always a possibility." That was all we needed to hear, that there's always a possibility. So we opted to hope for the best, and we hung in there.

My mother was the glue that held our family together, that made us as close as we were. She kept in touch with everyone. She was the kind of woman you could go to with anything, and she'd make you feel better about it, put it in perspective. She always made me feel that there was no obstacle I couldn't hurdle.

Whenever we came to visit her, we'd talk to her, share our day and share our thoughts. We weren't convinced that she was able to hear, but we just wanted to spend time with her. Then, one day, she opened up one eye and looked around. After a time she was able to open her other eye, but they

He never talked about death, about succumbing to the cancer. It was never discussed.

were not looking in the same direction. Through her own will, she was able to bring them together over a period of time. She could see, but she was never able to communicate or have control over any other muscles.

We didn't know what our mother could understand, but we realized that we should tell her that our father had died. If she had any consciousness at all, she would be able to make sense of who was there and who wasn't. We thought she might be wondering why our father wasn't there. Breaking the news to her that Dad was gone was hard.

My mother's condition was more severe and went on for longer than my dad's. She needed around-the-clock care. We checked her out of the hospital when the doctors came to the decision that no further advances were being made. We put her in a nursing home. My sisters, bless their hearts, were always there to make sure that she was getting the best treatment she could get. And I was there whenever possible. Months later, while still in the nursing home, my mother suffered the stroke that killed her. She was seventy when she died, and I was forty.

I SEE MYSELF BECOMING MY FATHER

I understand my father better now than I did when he was alive. He was a kind, generous, quiet man. He had a quiet strength that my sisters and I loved and respected. But as I was growing up, I didn't think that my father and I had anything in common.

Now I see myself becoming my father. I'll say something or make a hand gesture and think, *That's my dad.* And I understand his philosophy more now. Having raised two stepdaughters, I understand some of his difficulties and frustrations in raising children.

As the only son, I probably relate to the loss of my parents along the lines of how my father would relate to it. I see my sisters expressing sadness more, tears coming to their eyes, and talking more than I am able to. I get choked up when we talk about my parents. Sometimes I have those good cries. But I think I keep things inside more than my sisters do.

I try to emulate my parents as far as the things they unconsciously taught my sisters and me about being good human beings—just being considerate of others and never forgetting that we're all equal in this ball game. I don't care who it is, I don't look above or below anybody. I try to get on an even keel with everyone, and treat people respectfully, whether they're the doorman or janitor or the president of a corporation. That was what our parents instilled in us, and that goes a long way.

I understand my father better now than I did when he was alive.

I have kept some small things from my childhood that I remember being in the family house. Little knickknacks, figurines. My parents collected Hummel figurines, and my sisters and I distributed them among us. They will always remind us of Mom and Dad. When I was five or six years old, my parents made a little disc, a recording, of the two of them at the top of the Empire State Building. That recording has become near and dear to me. On it, you hear my young parents telling their children what it is like looking down from so high and how the people below look so small, like little ants. My dad said, in his German accent, "and windy, too." That's become something of a catchphrase in my family—"and *vindy,* too."

BEGINNING, MIDDLE, AND END

When you lose your parents, along with the sadness comes loneliness and a reevaluation of your place in life. After my parents died I developed an understanding that there's a beginning, middle, and end to everyone's life—a circular process of life. Your turn is going to come up, and it will be your children mourning for you someday. That's the way life is. You have to keep the memories of your parents in your heart and in your mind.

My parents are uppermost in my mind whenever I gain any recognition. I always include them in my thank-you speeches or make special mention of them. The first Emmy I won for *NYPD Blue* was for them. I knew they were looking down and were as proud as I was. I always think, *Gosh, I wish they were here to share this with me.* My wife and I have such an abundance of lucky fortune; we know what joy my parents would have had in sharing my success and experiences.

Recently we bought some property on a lake in Idaho that is exactly what my parents would have loved. My father was a wonderful fisherman. He used to live to go fishing. I walk around the lake property now and say, "Can you imagine Mom and Dad here? This would be heaven for them." I say to my wife, "Gee, we could have bought them a nice house out here. We could have had them with us, given them cars, taken them on wonderful trips." So they're never out of my memory. They are there with me, in every step I take.

Though I miss my parents dearly, I'm so glad that I miss them. If I didn't, it would mean that they didn't have as much of an impact on my life as they do. I would like to have the same sort of impact on our children.

Geraldine Ferraro

GERALDINE FERRARO
You're Going to Miss Your Parents for the Rest of Your Life

MY MOTHER WAS ALMOST eighty-five when she died. My father had died when I was eight. It wasn't easier just because my mother was older, and I was older, when she passed away. If you have a good relationship with your parents, I don't care how old they are, it hurts when they die.

Right after my mother died, I went away with my husband for a few weeks. When we arrived home, John went into the den and called his mother. I had nobody to call. From the time I was first married, whenever I walked into the house after being away, I would call my mother. I didn't know what to do. I was devastated.

I don't care how old they are, it hurts when they die.

You're going to miss your parents for the rest of your life. I still get misty thinking of mine. Even today I come home and say, "I really wish I could tell my mother that."

It's amazing how much I still miss them.

THE KID WITHOUT A FATHER

One morning, when I was eight years old, I woke up and went into my parents' bedroom, and was surprised to find my father still in bed. He was looking at me, and my mother said, "Gerry, leave the room." When my mother came out of the bedroom, she told me, "Daddy's gone to heaven." He had died of a heart attack.

I never went back in that room.

My father had always put his wife and children on a pedestal. He was a restaurant/bar owner, and owned a five-and-ten store with a huge toy department. I was spoiled; I had all the latest toys. I had a dollhouse with little lightbulbs, and something like sixty-two dolls. At about two o'clock in the afternoon, I would go meet my father at the restaurant, and he would take me to Shirley Temple movies. He would walk with me and hold my hand, and sometimes give me piggyback rides.

My father was a tall, strapping man, forty-four years old, and nobody knew he had a heart condition. After he died, I overheard my mother saying that if she had known, she would never have let him carry me upstairs. So for the longest time, I thought his death was my fault, because I let him give me piggyback rides.

We had a wake in our living room. I was overwhelmed by the smell of flowers in the house. For years I would be somewhere and all of a sudden, for no apparent reason, the smell would come back. I'd see the whole thing all over again: the people packed into our living room, the burial. We drove down to the cemetery, where my mother had already buried two of my brothers. One of my brothers died when he was three days old. My other brother, Gerard, was killed in an automobile accident when he was three years old. I am named after him.

People kept saying, "Your father was so young." But when you're eight years old, forty-four is not young at all.

After my father died, there was a void in my life. I was the kid without a father. My mother was running the five-and-ten and trying to get the restaurant sorted out. It was a difficult time. My father had been the one who managed the finances. When he died, my mother ended up with almost nothing. She had to sell the businesses and our house. We moved to the South Bronx, across the street from her sister, and my mother picked up a trade she'd had as a little girl, crochet beading. When we walked in the door of the apartment, I said, "It's so small." I'll never forget the hurt look on my mother's face. I ended up going to boarding school because she couldn't afford to pay somebody to take care of me, and my grandmother didn't want to come and help.

The nuns at the Catholic boarding school were not too pleased with me. I was in emotional pain; I missed my father and wanted to be with my mother. I was put in a dormitory with six sets of bunk beds in a room, and they made us go to bed at 7:00 PM. When I got into bed, I could hear the lonely whistle of the train coming up the Hudson River, and I cried myself to sleep every night.

If I get upset, I internalize it. I don't get crazed. If something terrible happens, I'm able to handle it. If you saw me you might say, "She's handling this very well." But it's all inside. When my father died, my brother, Carl, cried a lot. I didn't. Everybody said, "Poor Carl. He's really having a hard time." Well, my brother was perfectly alright after he got it out of his system.

One night, I got violently sick in my bed because I was so distraught about my father. I was on the top bunk and was too weak to move; I threw up everywhere. The sheets and bed were a mess.

If something terrible happens, I don't get crazed. But it's all inside.

The next morning the nun walked in and was livid because the whole place smelled. She made me get up and wash myself, and then she made me take my sheets and wash them in the sink as punishment. As I washed the sheets, I was gagging and dry heaving. I was so weak that finally they put me in the infirmary and called my mother.

My mother came to school and took me home. We never went back.

Many years later, during my freshman year of high school, there was a father-daughter dance. The girls wore long gowns, and the fathers wore tuxedos. It was a closed weekend, which meant that nobody could go home. When my mother heard that the school wouldn't let me go home, she called them and said, "What kind of cruelty is this?" They said, "Well, Mrs. Ferraro, she has to realize her father is dead." My mother said, "Realize her father is dead? She realizes it every day, and she has since she was eight years old. She realizes it every time she walks in the door and comes into a South Bronx apartment instead of a house."

After that, the boarding school changed the policy and allowed kids who didn't have fathers to go home for the weekend. Later, when I was a senior, I stayed—but as a hostess. One of the fathers asked me to dance. That father was Jackie Gleason.

The things my mother taught me are things you live with for a lifetime. She taught me how to be a survivor. She taught me the value of work. She taught me that doing well in school can mean a scholarship; it can lead to a college education and a good future. She wanted me to treat people with respect, no matter who they were. She also taught me basic things, like how to clean the house and how to iron. I can probably iron a man's shirt better than anybody.

My mother's ability to handle negatives prepared me for life. She made it perfectly clear that she was there to help me, but nobody was going to give me anything. I had to earn it. I also learned that life is full of disappointments, and you have to learn to handle them. If you make a mistake, don't brood about it. Deal with it and move on.

I really miss my father, but I don't think I would be the person I am today if he had lived. I don't think I would have been as strong or as resourceful. I would have stayed in Newburgh, New York and married somebody from West Point. I would not have become a prosecutor. I would not have been a congresswoman. I certainly never would have run for vice president of the United States. So, my father's dying, in a strange way, shows that good can come out of horrible things. My father's death made me stronger.

OUR ROLES REVERSED

When my mother was young, she had been a flapper and liked to smoke. She never smoked with my father; he didn't like it. But after he died she started smoking again. At that time I smoked, too. When my daughter, Donna, was five, I told my mother, "I don't want the kids to grow up seeing us smoke, because then they'll do it." She agreed, and I thought she gave it up too. She never smoked in front of me again.

In the summer of 1985, I was out on Fire Island for a weekend with Madeleine Albright, who was my foreign policy adviser on the 1984 presidential campaign. We had become good friends. I got a call from one of my mother's neighbors at two o'clock in the morning. She said, "Your mother is at the hospital. She's having trouble breathing." Madeleine said, "I'm going with you." We went across the water in my son's boat. When we got to the hospital, the doctor told me that it was emphysema, but that if my mother stopped smoking, she would be fine. "My mother doesn't smoke," I said. I turned to her and asked, "Do you?"

I didn't know. She didn't want to disappoint me, and she certainly didn't want to be nagged. My mother used to volunteer in my congressional office in the 78th District, and apparently she told my staff, "If you tell my daughter I smoke, I'm going to tell her what you do." She threatened them! My brother knew and never told me. My husband and kids never told me.

As we got older, our roles reversed in many ways. She had taken care of me, and now it was my turn. From 1985 to 1990, she was in a steady decline. If it was windy, she couldn't breathe. And she was very frail. I became her protector and provider. I would drive her to the doctor and make sure that I knew what he was doing, make sure everything was under control. I took her everywhere. It wasn't a burden; it wasn't even payback. I loved her. I took one day off a week to spend time with her. I never wanted to regret that I didn't. After she was in the hospital for the last time, she came home with me for seven weeks, and I just stayed home. As long as she needed me to be there, I was there. This was what I wanted to do—for us.

When my mother went into the hospital for the last time, when she was eighty-four, they asked a series of questions to determine her lucidity. "Did you graduate from high school?" the nurse asked. My mother said, "No, I didn't. But I graduated from elementary school." Then she looked down at her hands and said, "Big deal." It dawned on me then that this incredible woman had gone through life thinking she was nothing because she'd had to quit school in the eighth grade. So I put my arms around her and said, "You'd better believe it's a big deal. Do you know anybody else, male or female, who can say, 'My daughter ran for vice president of the United States'?" She laughed and said, "No."

Nobody had greater confidence in me than my mother. She always said, "My daughter is going to be famous." When Walter Mondale asked me to be his running mate, my mother was the first person I called after my husband. She was so excited. She thought that I could do anything. She was probably the only person in the country who was surprised that we didn't win.

When I got the nomination, I couldn't help but think of my father. He would have been stunned and proud; he was a good American. He loved Italy, and loved his parents, but America was his life.

I WANT MY CHILDREN TO REMEMBER

After my mother died, there were certain things I couldn't get rid of. When my daughter Donna got married in 1989, my mother had osteoporosis, so I had to find her a suit and get it altered to fit. She only wore it that one time. After she died I kept it; I couldn't throw it away. Even when I moved, I took it with me. I also have some of my mother's kitchen towels. I keep them in a drawer; the smell reminds me of her. Every once in a while, I take them out to see if the smell is still there.

My father gave my mother a ring right before he died, and after she died I had it made into earrings. I wear them a lot. One day I'll use other pieces of my mother's jewelry to make some things for my daughters. I also have the diamond watch my father gave her when they got married. I wear it when I go to really fancy events.

As for my father, I have his picture on my nightstand. I've also kept his American flag. He used to fly it constantly. It is small and tattered, but it's his. Maybe I'll have them bury me with it.

My diagnosis of multiple myeloma eight years ago gave me a sudden awareness of mortality. They told me I had three to five years to live. At the time I thought, *If I live until the end of that prognosis, sixty-eight will be my last birthday. What do I want to do with my remaining five years?*

My children have stepped in. At a certain point, as I found with my mother, you go from taking care of your children to having them take care of you. My children are as close to me as I was to my mother, but I am not as dependent on them because I have a husband. John goes everywhere I do for the treatment of my cancer. It makes me sad that my mother didn't have that.

I try to help my children remember their grandparents. I'm so glad that they got to know my mother. I appreciate the values and the love she gave them; they'll always have a little piece of her. I want them to remember the holidays she valued. I want them to remember who she was.

You hope that when you bury a parent, whatever strands you got from them, you'll transfer to your children. You'll bring up your children knowing about your relationship with your own parents. I think that's important to do.

It's important to recognize the inevitable—that you will some-day be without both parents. That's the cycle of life. So while your parents are alive, enjoy them. Then, when you lose them, you can say you don't have regrets. I want my children to be able to grieve, and then ultimately accept a time when they will not have my husband and me.

Ice-T

ICE-T
I Must Stand

I'VE ALWAYS FELT LIKE an outsider. Every Thanksgiving, every Christmas, it was me, sitting at someone else's table. It was this vibe like when you're over at somebody's house and they're whispering in the kitchen, "*Why is he here?*"

I came into life so hard that when I see other adults who say they need or want their parents, it seems corny to me. When there's nobody to hug you when you cry, eventually you stop crying. I think that's how I ended up getting called "Ice."

When people talk about their mothers and fathers, they talk about them with a lot of love in their hearts. I never had anybody like that in my life that I can remember. Eventually you detach from the need for those particular emotions you've never gotten. So you don't need love. You don't need Christmas or other holidays. You don't need any of it.

THEY WERE TRYING TO PROTECT ME
My mother passed away when I was in third grade. I was there when

she died. We were sitting together, watching *Batman* on TV. She tilted her head back and started to breathe heavily; she was having a heart attack. My father knew something was happening, and he told me to go next door to our neighbors'. I was there when the ambulance came.

Later that night, when my father told me, "Your mother passed away," I didn't even cry. I was an only child, almost eight years old. My mother was relatively young—in her thirties. I thought, "Okay. My mother's dead, I guess." It didn't really hit me. It was more like, "So what's next? What does this mean?"

I didn't go to the funeral. I was shuttled to my aunt's—my father's sister, who lived behind us. We lived in Summit, New Jersey, and our back yards connected. My aunt kept me out of the mix. I didn't have anything to do with the preparations. It was like nothing had really happened. Now I realize they were trying to protect me, but at the time it was hard to understand.

I've always felt like an outsider.

From that point on, I never had a motherly presence in my life. All the normal things mothers do, like hugging you and showing you affection, were lacking in my life. My father was a cold cat. He worked and provided, and that was pretty much it. No kisses, no hugs. But I knew he was there.

Four years later, when I was in the seventh grade, I was called down to the principal's office. I knew I hadn't done anything, so obviously it was something about my father. When I got there, the vibe was different; everybody had a funny face. They said, "You need to sit down. Your father passed." He'd had a heart attack, just like my mother. I thought, *Why was I dealt this card? Who do I panic to? Do I cry to the people at this school? What do I do?*

It was the same thing as when my mother died. Everybody kept me away from the funeral preparations, and I stayed at my aunt's house. I didn't go to my dad's funeral. I don't even know where my parents are buried.

I thought my aunt in New Jersey would take care of me. I'd been living with her pretty much already. She said, "We're going to deal with it. Everything's going to be okay." As it turned out, her plan was to send me to Los Angeles to live with my father's other sister. They said she was in a better situation; she already had two boys. I wasn't happy about it. I thought I was going for the summer, but then all my clothes showed up. I didn't want to stay.

That was the first time I was emotional. I felt more connected to my aunt in New Jersey, and I missed my friends. Why would I want to live in Los Angeles, a place I didn't know anything about? On top of that, my aunt in California had this attitude like "I'm going to take care of you because I have to." I wasn't welcome, but I had to stay there. I mean, what are you going to do? You're just a kid.

I was bitter with my people from New Jersey. After I called them crying, they decided, "Let's not take his phone calls anymore and let him just deal with it." I held that against them. I was out in California with this screwed-up aunt, who also happened to be an alcoholic. It was a bad situation. I never talked to them again.

When my mother passed, I felt like, *Okay, I've still got somebody. I'm not alone.* But when my father passed, I knew I was by myself. I thought, *Who is responsible for me? Who is supposed to care about me now?*

I was with my aunt in California until I was seventeen. I graduated from high school with what they called a "twenty-week report card," which means that if you have enough credits, you can finish halfway through the year. I told my aunt, "Look, the government is giving you $250 a month for me. Give me that and I'm out." At that point we were at odds; I was in gangs and everything else, looking for some type of family. She signed the check over to me and said, "You'll be back. You'll never survive." I walked out of her door with the clothes on my back, and I never saw her again.

When there's nobody to hug you when you cry, eventually you stop crying.

MY FRIENDS BECAME MY FAMILY

As soon as my father died, I immediately felt older. You feel older as soon as you realize there's nobody to hear your cries. After my parents died, I took it out on myself. Not physically—mentally. You turn your head into a brick. And you think, "What could possibly happen to me next? So it's almost like, "Let me just live my life, and if I get killed, I get killed." That's when you become a dangerous person.

It's a lonely life having no love. Even if you don't know about love, you want to experience it. That's where gangs fit in. It's all about having someone say, "No matter what, nothing is ever going to happen to you. We got you. It's what you wish you got from your parents, but you didn't. There are a lot of negatives that go along with gangs, but there are a lot of positives, too. So I connected. I found allegiance with my friends. My friends became my family.

Now, I have a son and a daughter, and I love them. I'm definitely down for them. But I don't have all the love mechanisms that you have if you learn love from your family. If you've never seen it, you don't have it. I know my kids want it, but I don't really know how to give it. They know I love them, though. If they need me, I'm there.

My daughter, Letesha, was born when I was in high school. At the time, I wanted a kid, because I was by myself. But then it dawned on me, after helping to raise her for about three years, that the lifestyle I was living wasn't conducive to having a child. And her mother didn't need me; she needed to get married and go on with her life. So I used my brains. I handed my daughter back to her

I found allegiance with my friends. My friends became my family.

mother. I was there for her; there was nothing she didn't have. But I kind of silently laid in the cut until she was fourteen or fifteen. I'm such a strong father figure; I knew there was never going to be a guy who could come around and discipline Letesha if I stayed in the picture.

Letesha now lives in Atlanta and has three children of her own. My fourteen-year-old son, Little Ice, lives in L.A. I have good relationships with them. And my wife, Coco, gets along with everybody. They all love Coco. Somehow or another I have kind of started to weave something together that looks like a family.

In my last relationship, with my son's mother, I never dealt with her family. I refused to go to Christmases or Thanksgivings. I just would not do it. With Coco, I'm more emotional. Her family is special. They're the nicest people I've ever met. And they have a seamless willingness to accept people into their house. I told Coco this year I would really like to have our own table and invite people to us. I want to work on my own family.

I don't think about my father or even my mother when I'm onstage. I think more about Little Ice. I think about him being proud. I know he says, "My dad is Ice-T." His friends get a look at me and are like, "That's your dad?"

It was only recently that Coco and I were married. It's hard to trust that when you give yourself up to love, it won't be taken away from you like everything else. You're afraid to fall truly in love because you don't want something to happen. You cross your fingers every day.

I DON'T THINK I'LL EVER SEE MY PARENTS AGAIN

I have nothing that belonged to my parents. I don't even have a picture of them. My daughter stays in contact with my aunt in New Jersey and has gotten pictures of me as a baby. But I haven't seen them. I don't really have a need to see that stuff. My childhood is pretty much blocked out. I used to have photo books, and kept them in a car because I lost my apartment. And then my car got towed and all the stuff was stolen.

All my art comes from the struggle, from the times I sat alone and tried to figure out what was going on.

My parents are in my head. Now that I am older, it's one of the reasons I'm glad I didn't go to their funerals. I really remember my mother alive. I remember how she looked, and I remember sitting in her lap. I remember my dad laughing. I remember my dad put me in the back of the car and we got White Castle burgers. I don't remember him in a box.

I don't think I'll ever see my parents again. I think when it's a wrap, it's a wrap.

When I die, I don't want a funeral with my body present. If they want to have a service and talk about me, fine, but I don't want people to walk by and look at me. I know there are going to be a lot of fake people who weren't really there in my life. I don't need that last procession walking by me. And I also don't want my death to make anybody stagnate. Mourn for me, but then keep it moving.

MY PARENTS' DEATHS TURNED OUT TO BE A BLESSING

I believe that maturity is the accumulation of negative experiences. When you're young, you think, "I should always have a roof over my head and someplace to eat. I should always have somebody to take care of me when I'm sick," because your parents give you that. This is the illusion of life. When you become an adult, you realize that if you don't work, you don't eat. And just because someone told you they love you doesn't mean they won't leave you. And life starts to hit you. You learn.

When you come from where I came from, the only positive thing you have is in front of you. You get to the point where you say, "If I want to be happy, I've got to make myself happy." I don't think it's healthy to focus backward.

I've had a lot of experience with death. And you just have to write it off as part of the game. Life has to go on. I'm not really a spiritual person; I'm not connected to a religion. But I do believe there is karma. I believe there is some energy going on. It's all about looking at today and being happy and trying to enjoy it, and surrounding yourself with people who are trying to do the same thing.

My parents' deaths turned out to be a blessing. I would not have become the person I am today if they had lived. I would have just gone into the fabric of America, running a computer company or something. I would be no one. All my art comes from the struggle, from the times I sat alone and tried to figure out what was going on. It comes from the trouble I've been through, the trial and error, the mistakes.

Because of all my bad experiences, I have something to tell. I think that's what people get from my music. I say what's on my mind, and there's a lot of anger there. I'm not going to pull a punch.

> *Just a kid, moms died when I was seven*
> *Pops died, eleven, what's up with heaven?*
> *It's hell when you're an orphan at a early age*
> *This impressionable stage, no love breeds rage*
> *In the heart of a child who never knew his roots*
> *Looked up to pimps and to hustlers in the eelskin boots . . .*

—ICE-T, "I MUST STAND"

I think my parents would be proud of me. But I don't think anybody out there would be too surprised at what I've done. You take a kid, drop him the middle of the water, he's either going to sink or swim; it's one or the other. If he swims, he's probably going to be a good swimmer.

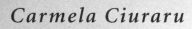

Carmela Ciuraru

CARMELA CIURARU
Art, Music, and Books Have Saved My Life

AFTER MY DAD DIED, I put all of my parents' belongings into storage. I shut the lock and never went back. The unit is full, and it's five feet wide by five feet deep, and eight feet tall. I was twenty-one when I put everything in there, and now I'm in my thirties. It's a big waste of money, and I know I need to deal with it—I just haven't felt ready. It's going to be like opening a vault, and it's going to be extremely painful. It's also a matter of time. I'm so busy, and the idea of leaving New York and going down to Maryland to figure out what I should do with everything—I just can't do it yet. But it makes me feel better knowing it's there.

I DIDN'T HAVE A GOOD GOODBYE

My mom had breast cancer throughout my childhood, but she actually died from an aneurysm when I was a junior in high school. We were living in Houston, and I had stayed over at a friend's house, and came back the next day and couldn't get into the house. I was knocking on the door frantically, and I heard my dogs inside.

I finally got in through the back door and found her on the couch, unconscious. I didn't know what was wrong. I called the neighbors, the hospital, and my dad. My father was in Maryland at the time, lining up a new job and a new house for us to move into a few weeks later. I was freaked out and upset, but I knew I had to act fast. I was alone with her and had to deal with it.

I rode with my mother in the ambulance to the hospital. She was forty-one and never recovered consciousness. I felt helpless and terrified. I kept thinking, there's got to be a way for this to be okay.

I didn't have a good goodbye with my mother. And I think that's always been hard for me.

In painful moments, I think that if I had been there to help her get to the hospital sooner, she might have lived. But people say there was nothing I could've done. I'll never know. You'd like to think you could have done something.

My mother's funeral was very small. My father kept me out of all the planning. My parents were both Romanian, and though I don't blame him at all, I think he had an immigrant, old-school way of dealing with things. I was a kid, his daughter, and I don't think it would have occurred to him to talk to me about what was going to happen with my mother's funeral.

After my mother died, my father tried to get closer to me. He was always trying, and I was always rejecting his efforts. I felt like my dad didn't understand me. I believe now I must have been angry at him—not in a rational way, but "Oh, my mom is gone—and you're the one I'm left with." And not only was I dealing with losing my mom, but I was also being ripped away to Maryland. The pain of moving aggravated the whole thing. I also remember being very upset because we had to give away my dogs. My father didn't know how to deal with bringing them from Houston to Maryland, so I lost them too.

I didn't like the kids at my new school in Maryland, either. I felt isolated and disconnected from my peers; they were into having a good time and drinking, and I didn't want anything to do with that. I couldn't relate to them because I was in a different place entirely. I remember eating lunch by myself most days. I was extremely alone and it was very painful.

I did work for my school newspaper, which I really liked. I felt comfortable there. One day, when I covered a public-school-employee strike, Katie Couric was there, covering it as a local *I didn't have a good* TV reporter. I asked her if she *goodbye with my mother.* would talk to my journalism class, which she did. She's been like an older sister to me ever since. In high school, I was always at Katie's house; I would sleep over or go to her place after school. I don't have any siblings, so spending time with her helped me a lot.

Anything you could think of, I would love to say to my mother now. Just mundane things I would love to share with her. In terms of the big stuff, things I accomplish or wonderful things in my life—they've been bittersweet because I haven't been able to share them with her. Every time something great has happened—like when I got into Columbia University for graduate school—I wanted to tell her and tell my father, and I couldn't. And every accomplishment I've had—it's been bittersweet, because they weren't around to see it.

YOU'RE NEVER FINISHED

I was twenty when my dad was diagnosed with colon cancer. He was fifty-seven. I don't remember the conversation where my father told me it was cancer; I only remember him telling me, at first, the symptoms: I'm having trouble with this, I'm having trouble with that; I'm going to go to the doctor. I think I was in denial. It never occurred to me that I could lose both parents. Some days I still can't believe they're both gone.

At twenty-one, I was dealing with exceptionally heavy stuff. I had to sell the house and move everything out.

My father went to a treatment program at the National Institutes of Health. I was happy about that. It was a harsh treatment, but it was good. It was experimental and cutting-edge, but it took quite a toll on his body.

I liked my father's doctor. I did what I had to do to help my dad when he was sick. I must have wanted to make up for not having been able to help my mom. Since I was older and a little more mature, I just wanted to give him whatever I could, and I did.

I was at George Mason University at the time and took time off to care for him. It was kind of perfect, in the sense of a loss, because I got to be there with him when he was getting sicker, and even when he died. That was really intense. Those final minutes are in my head very clearly, as if they happened yesterday.

We got really close before he died, and I spent a lot of time with him. He loved that I wrote for the university newspaper, and he loved reading my articles. I knew he was proud of me, which was comforting. I was able to say everything that I wanted to say to him. You're never finished, of course, but he certainly knew that I loved him. And I knew that he loved me, as well.

I BELIEVE IN PAMPERING YOURSELF

My dad tried to make sure I'd be okay after he died. He took care of his will and had a really nice lawyer, and the lawyer helped me make decisions. At twenty-one, I was dealing with exceptionally heavy stuff. I had to sell the house and move everything out; it didn't occur to me to ask anyone for help. Nobody offered, so I was moving hundred-pound chairs by myself. I carried them to a van and took them to that storage facility. When I think back on what I did, it seems crazy now that I emptied that entire house by myself. But when you're young, you don't know better, and you do foolish things.

I took the stuff that was most meaningful to me. The rest I had to let go because I didn't have anywhere for it to go. Doing that was overwhelming and confusing, and I was too exhausted to know whether I was handling everything as I should.

My dad had an encyclopedic knowledge of opera and classical music. I developed a love of classical music myself, so I took those records with me. And I took some of his clothes. He was an avid photographer, so I took his photographs and some books. I also made sure to take the first typewriter my mother gave me. I doubt if it still works. That was a precious object to me, because I love writing. I also have some of my mother's jewelry and clothes.

After my father died, it hit me that I was truly alone in the world, with no other family. There was so much that I needed to learn and figure out for myself about becoming an adult. And I felt so far behind, compared with my friends.

I've spent a lot of holidays by myself. It used to set off panic in me as soon as holidays started coming around every year. My friends would say casually, "Oh, you can come to my family's house for Christmas or Thanksgiving," but then they would forget, or never call to follow up. So I finally started making holidays for myself, going away to cool places so I wouldn't feel so miserable and alone. I would fly to Miami, in the eighty-degree sunshine, and stay in a lovely hotel and swim in the ocean and have a great time. What I learned is how to make my own holidays—to treat myself. I believe very much in pampering yourself, and I don't make any excuses about it. If I want to do something, I'm going to treat myself and enjoy it.

I feel defined by loss in every way.

Even on the anniversaries of my parents' deaths, I try to do something nice for myself—and of course, that doesn't always have to involve spending money—but if you've endured traumatic loss, it's important not to deprive yourself.

GRIEF MAKES YOU GREEDY

I do feel defined by loss in every way—my lack of confidence, my confidence. My lack of self-esteem, my self-esteem. Everything comes from the loss, and it comes out in unpredictable ways. It has shaped my sensibility, my interests, my sense of humor— everything, absolutely. Sometimes it has adversely affected my relationships with other people, my friendships, my focus and discipline—and that's been a huge regret of mine. Yet sometimes I have incredible drive that comes from knowing how quickly life can be cut short.

I read once that grief makes you greedy. Instead of grief making you put everything in perspective, and thinking, *Oh, that's no big deal, I've lost my parents; I can deal with that,* it kind of magnifies everything, so that it's hugely out of proportion—big. I think that's been hard for my friends, because it's made me want more, not less. More love. There's never enough. People don't know how to give you what you need, so you have to learn to turn inward for that kind of affection.

My friends don't always understand why I am still sad. I should be fine now; it's been years. Some days I am totally fine, and other times it's hard to get through the day. I think people need to be more sensitive to the fact that the loss remains active for the rest of your life. It doesn't go away; it just changes.

FIND SOMETHING THAT WILL MAKE YOU STRONG

You learn how strong you are in times of loss. Something gets you through and makes you more resilient, and you don't know what that is, but it's a nice discovery, learning what you are capable of enduring. You also begin to appreciate all the good stuff more—going to a museum, cooking a great meal. Loss also makes you appreciate your good friends, the people you love. I always try to tell people how I feel. They could be gone the next day, or I could.

My dad enjoyed learning. He taught himself photography, and he learned to appreciate classical music on his own. I inherited that from him. For instance, I wanted to learn art, so I took a drawing class; I studied violin because I wanted to become more immersed in classical music. Those are things my dad would have done, too.

As clichéd as it is, time has been the biggest help. Over time you understand more about who you are, and what support systems you have, and you're more comfortable in your own skin. I suspect that as I get into my forties, I'll feel even more okay.

Art, music, and books have saved my life. As a comfort, as a companion, as a source of wisdom—in a way that religion never has. I love Judaism as an idea, and I went through periods of finding it as a comfort, between my mother dying and my father dying, and then eventually I didn't anymore. I'm pretty comfortably atheistic now—happily so. Part of the reason is that I associate religion with my family and going to synagogue with them. So the idea of doing that on my own now is very painful; it doesn't feel right. So over time, I've achieved my own way of finding peace. If I'm feeling sad, instead of going to synagogue, I'll go to a bookstore and browse for hours. Or I'll go to the Metropolitan Museum of Art, or MoMA [the Museum of Modern Art]. I stand in front of the paintings and feel completely absorbed. And I always feel stronger when I walk out of the building.

Music helps me, too. Aside from the usual angst-ridden pop songs when I was younger, there was classical music that I found comforting, especially Bach's Cello Suite no. 5 in C Minor, and Beethoven's late string quartets.

Poetry has also been hugely important in my life. A poem can speak to you in a way that a person can't, and it can say all the right things. The poems I love are not happy poems. They're sad poems. Hearing someone else express the same thing I'm feeling is what's comforting. It doesn't really help me to read a poem about being happy. The poet Louise Glück deals with loss quite a lot, and for years I carried her books around with me like Bibles. Her poems have provided me with a great deal of solace—more than just about any other contemporary poet has.

It's not going to be music or words for everyone. For other people, maybe it's sports or exercise. But it's crucial to have something—an interest that has nothing to do with anyone else and is completely private.

You've got to find something that will make you strong.

Dana Buchman

DANA BUCHMAN
No Barrier Between You and Death

BOTH OF MY PARENTS died quickly, and I wasn't expecting it. You never get to say enough goodbyes. My father died when I was thirty and my mother when I was forty-three. People in my family live to be ninety-seven, so my parents died relatively young. After my mother died, it felt as if so much was changing. The house we grew up in was sold. Her funeral was in the church I grew up in, and I knew it was probably the last time I'd be there. I felt older, face-to-face with my own mortality. I felt grief for my mother, grief for me, grief for time passing, and the sense that I was next. You always imagine that your parents will go first, and then, when they're gone, there's no barrier between you and death.

THE NEWS TOOK MY BREATH AWAY

I grew up in Memphis in a close-knit, nurturing family. We had a family dinner every night and spent a lot of time together. When I was eleven, my father walked with me to Sears, Roebuck to buy my first sewing machine. I got a very fancy, top-of-the-line one that could do anything. I had expressed interest in designing; my grandmother sewed, and I spent a lot of time with her. My parents were very encouraging. My dad made a point of being awestruck, no matter what I did. That was a given. I could count on it. He'd say, "You're so smart, you're beautiful, you're creative."

When I left Memphis at seventeen to go to college, I talked to my parents at least twice a week. After college I went to the Rhode Island School of Design and then to England to study fashion. My parents said, "Whatever you'd like to do is fine with us," which is a nice voice to have in your head. Once I was working, I talked to them almost every day. They have always been a big support.

When my father died, I was at my first job in New York City, as an assistant in a fashion company. It was different than anywhere I'd ever been—a little rough around the edges—and I loved it. My mother called me at work and burst into tears. I was in the sample room, surrounded by pattern-makers and sewers from all over the world. My sixty-four-year-old father had had a stroke. The news took my breath away. Everything around me disappeared, and my attention telescoped to the phone call.

My mother said, "You don't have to come now," but she knew I'd come. I flew home to Memphis and went straight to the hospital. When I got to my dad's bedside, he couldn't speak, but he indicated that I should stand up straight. He had been a captain in the U.S. Army and was always advocating a straight posture. To this day, I have very good posture. So I knew it was a loving gesture, as if he were saying, "I'm still here. I'm still the same me."

I adored my father. It felt so good to be with him. I stayed a few days, and then it looked like he was stable, so I went back to New York. But a week later I got a call that he'd had another stroke. My brother and sister and I came home.

My dad was in intensive care, on a respirator, and wasn't able to communicate with us. It was shocking; I had never seen him helpless. He had always been strong and gentle, *Everything around me disappeared, and my attention telescoped to the phone call.* and so alive. Now there was a big tube in his throat, and it made a loud noise. I went up and took his hand, and that made it clear that he was still my father. But he was not mentally present.

I stayed at my mother's house, and one night the hospital called and told us to come. They didn't tell us over the phone that he was dying, but we knew. We got dressed quietly and went to the hospital, all of us. By the time we arrived, he was already gone.

Illness and death simplify things. There was a great feeling of solidarity among the siblings. The rallying around of our extended family gave us strength. We felt surrounded by love; it was almost like a primal ritual, the gathering in of the clan against the saber-toothed tiger.

After my father died we all took a walk, my two siblings, my mother, and me. My family has always been big on walks. Now it felt ritualistic, almost like paying tribute to him.

Over the next few months, I watched my mother. She was very sad, very emotional, but she wasn't falling apart. And that was helpful to see. My parents had had a very happy marriage for over forty years. My maternal grandmother had given them a cow pasture to build their house on, and they built it together. After my dad died, my mother was alone in the house. She had no intention of moving. She didn't believe in going to any kind of support group; it wasn't her thing. What she did was start traveling with me on business trips. She would come with me to Italy or Asia, and we'd stay in beautiful hotels. We got very close. The plane ride became part of the fun; I was so jaded by then, and she enjoyed having all the perks. I saw it through new eyes.

It made me proud to have her there, seeing me become a success.

My mom got to see more of my professional life than my dad did. She loved it. She went on personal appearances with me, to department stores in different cities. She added richness to my business trips. It made me proud to have her there, seeing me become a success. She didn't always like the clothes, and I had to tell her, "If you don't love something, you don't have to comment at the store! Tell me later." She enjoyed being outspoken. She was always very honest, a straight talker.

My mother was alone for three years. She would call, and I'd be in meetings with twenty people, and she'd want to talk about the tomatoes growing in her garden and the things that happened in her day. Then she met a man from Ireland, and we found out that he owned a castle estate there. She really enjoyed being with him, and I was so glad. It wasn't a betrayal of my father; it was what he would have wanted.

MY MOTHER'S GARDEN

My sister was with my mother when she died. They were going on a trip in the car. As my sister was backing the car down the driveway, my mother took a long look back at her beautiful garden. Once they were on the road, she fell asleep. My sister was talking to her and finally realized something was wrong. She tried to wake my mother up and couldn't, so she took her to the hospital. They tried to revive her, but she was gone. It was her heart. My mother was seventy-eight. If you have to go, how lovely just to be with your daughter and go to sleep.

After the funeral I walked around my mother's garden. It had never looked better. There was a beautiful plant I'd never seen before. It was soft and willowy and huge, and looked like a dandelion the size of a basketball. It was like the garden was honoring her. I later took some of her plants and replanted them in my garden.

The actual experience of my mother's death was devastating. I cried for days. I just walked around with tears streaming down my face. By the time she died, I was forty-three, and my children had gotten to know her. Watching my two teenage daughters deal with the reality of her death made the whole process that much more difficult for me. I wish my parents were here for them. As I go through each life stage with my girls, I can hear the conversations I had with my mother when I was their age. Sometimes I actually say things she might have said. I hear my parents' voices a lot. My memories, and their voices, are very alive.

My parents are also alive in the work I do and the clothes I design. The philosophy of my clothes comes, in part, from being their child. My mother was a timeless dresser. She wore clothes that were a little bit tailored, but always very feminine. My clothes are not designed as status symbols. I don't have my initials all over them. They're designed to fit your life, make you feel beautiful, and transcend the latest fads.

As I get older, I think of things I wish I'd asked or said to them. I wish I'd asked them more about life's different stages: What was it like when they were teenagers? What were dating, young courtship, and marriage in the 1950s like? I never had the guts. I wasn't mature enough to know that I should ask the questions.

Sometimes with your parents, you think you shouldn't ask things—but you should. You should push it and ask. I wish I had heard more.

THE BIG THING THAT HELPED

Losing both parents is very different than losing one parent. It's wrenching. But you've got to go on. You might as well; we'll join them sometime. That's what I think—that I'm going to find out whether I'll get to see them when I die. I fly a lot for work, and while I am not a religious person, I imagine when I'm above the clouds that I am with them. It's not truly a religious experience, but it's something. It's a feeling that what comes next can't just be nothing.

I think time is a big healer. Everybody finds their own way to get through the hurt. The ache in my heart for my father has faded a little. It's not as constant. My mother bubbles up in my mind at least once a week. It might be because I have girls, and they knew my mother. My father died before I met my husband, Tom, and had children. That's a great sadness for me. The two most important men in my life never got to meet.

It seems like death is the elephant in the room. In polite company you don't spend a lot of time talking about the most important thing that's going to happen to you. Death is not considered a seemly topic of conversation, but I think talking is important. For me, talking to people and turning to

> *Death is not considered a seemly topic of conversation, but I think talking is important.*

friends, was the big thing that helped: talking about my parents and listening to others who'd lost family members. It also helped to write down memories I didn't want to forget.

I found it helpful, too, to have some of my parents' personal things. While nothing will bring them back, these mementos are important. Things that have my parents' smell, or can jog a memory. My mother wasn't a big "thing" person, but when she died, I let each of my girls pick out a small memento that belonged to her. For myself, I have some glass figurines, paintings, and a pincushion that for the longest time smelled like her drawer. I have an old bottle of Shalimar perfume that evokes her. My father always wore classic Brooks Brothers ties, and I kept one of them. I have his army hat and all of his military bars. I also kept a film he shot when he was on the Galápagos Islands in World War II. I have a whole wall of photographs of my family and my husband's family, and I tell my daughters stories about them. I keep all of these things in my home, and in my heart.

LESSONS FROM THEIR DEATHS

There's not a day that goes by that something my parents taught me doesn't resurface. Even lessons from their deaths have been an important part of my personal growth. I feel like I can be a better friend now that I've been through this, because I know how incredibly painful it is. I am more empathetic toward what other people might be going through. I talk to my daughters openly about death and whether they will ever see my parents again. Despite these positive aspects, though, death still terrifies me. It is strikingly final.

Pamela Redmond Satran

PAMELA REDMOND SATRAN
Unresolved Issues

MY MOTHER WASN'T an easy person to get along with in the best of times. And in the worst of times, it was just horrible. She was mercurial. Even as a little girl, I didn't have a good relationship with her.

I was thirty when she died. I had just become a mother myself; my daughter was a year old. My mother had rheumatoid arthritis and had been bedridden and sick from the time I was in high school. She was severely crippled; her hands were claws, her feet were twisted up, and she couldn't really walk. She was in a wheelchair. Her back was hunched over, which caused problems with her breathing. She was sick for seventeen years, and it got progressively worse.

I was working at *Glamour* magazine as a fashion editor when my dad called me to tell me the news. My mother was sixty-one. I was stunned, which I think is always the reaction to death, no matter how much you anticipate it. I went into the office of the editor-in-chief, who wasn't even there at the time. Though she wasn't a motherly person, she was a legendary editor whom young women looked up to. I had an impulse to connect with her. I walked into her office and told her assistant, "My mother died." I started sobbing. Her poor assistant—what was she going to do? Put her arms around me? I ended up just going home.

I was thrown by how devastated I was by my mother's death, I think because I had so many unresolved issues with her. I was full of regrets. I became obsessed with the word "never." *Never, never, never.* I would never have the chance to make it good with her, to get beyond all the pain and anger. When my mother was alive, it never seemed possible to resolve things. We were so alienated from each other. It wasn't like we'd been close when I was a little kid, and then when she got sick, it became difficult. It was always difficult. There was nothing to go back to.

I would never have the chance to make it good with her, to get beyond all the pain and anger.

My mother had been in the middle of all of our lives in a negative way. I feel bad—you're not supposed to speak ill of the dead. But it's all too tempting to romanticize someone after they die. You know how when someone who's a real jerk dies, and everybody starts talking about what a good person they were?

I understand that my mother had a lot of serious problems and needed more help in her life. But she made us all very unhappy. We were able to have much happier lives when she was gone. She was a narcissist. After she got sick and my father was taking care of her, she demanded that all his attention be on her, that everybody's attention be on her. She wouldn't let him talk to me on the phone unless she was also on the line. If she heard us talking, she would start yelling from her bed, "Get off the phone. Who is that?" He was afraid to talk to me, because he'd have to pay for it with her anger.

Once you lose one parent, you know what the finality of death feels like. Anything short of that is so much better. I feel that maybe if I'd had more of a consciousness of the absoluteness of death, I might have tried harder to reconcile with my mother.

KIND OF BEAUTIFUL

My father's death was easier for me than my mother's, in part because I was thirty-eight years old and more experienced, but primarily because my relationship with him was more positive. I had the relationship with him that I wanted to have.

My dad died of emphysema. He went into the hospital and the doctors said, "This isn't serious. We're just regulating his oxygen. He's going to be fine." Two days later, the doctors said, "It's not fine." I was living in England, and my brother called and told me I had to come back right then. I came home, and my dad was in the hospital. Even though he was only semiconscious, he was still alive. I could still sit next to him and hold his hand. He was still my dad. That made me happy, even in the midst of sadness. I knew it was better than I was going to feel soon.

The last thing he said me to me was, "I love you." It was also the last thing I said to him. I felt so close to him. It was so different than it had been with my mother; I didn't feel there was anything left unsaid or undone.

There was so much about my dad's death that felt resolved and kind of beautiful. He wanted to be cremated, and we threw his ashes in his favorite trout stream in upstate New York. The trout stream was our idea, but we felt that he would have loved it. We had fished and camped with him there. When we threw his ashes in the stream, surrounded by mountains and water and fish, it was a great feeling. We felt like, *This is right. This is good.*

I had always wanted a third child, and my husband didn't; he felt two was just fine. But we both had the same reaction when my dad died, which was, "Let's make a baby." I was pregnant three weeks later, and my son Owen was born nine months after that. So very quickly, in a knee-jerk way, I put a new person in my family. I think I was trying to feel less alone.

I grew up Catholic, but I feel that the Jewish year of mourning is timed to an internal rhythm—that after a year, you are ready to let go. Having a boy the following summer—perhaps especially a boy—was a great event near the end of that year of mourning for my father.

AN ALONENESS I HADN'T FELT BEFORE

I felt more pain when my mother died than when my dad died. I think that the more difficult the relationship, the more pain you're going to feel. You need to accept that dichotomy. My mother was an angry and controlling person and it was certainly freeing to be without that. But to say that once a parent dies, it's over—it's not over. Especially with a difficult parent.

When my father died, I retreated into myself. I had been self-sufficient for a long time, so I didn't let other people in that much. Because my friends and I were younger then, I felt that most of them hadn't been through what I was going through, and that they really couldn't fathom it.

You can never really understand another person's loss. When an adult loses a parent, I think there's a sense of, "Well, she was sick. She's in a better place." Or, "He was getting older; it was his time"—that it was supposed to happen, so it shouldn't be that painful. And maybe I had the sense myself that I shouldn't be in so much pain. I had friends who lost both parents who weren't in so much agony. I was thinking, "Am I screwed up, or are they? They cried for a week or two, and now they say they're okay. What's wrong with me?"

I think you have to let yourself feel the pain that you're going to feel. It isn't useful to try not to feel it, to medicate it away, or chastise yourself for it, or repress it. You're going to feel it sooner or later anyway. You just have to let yourself feel whatever you feel, however painful and horrible it is.

When my dad died, I felt an aloneness I hadn't felt before. It's hugely different to lose both parents than to just lose one. The experience of orphanhood is powerful, even if you're an adult who doesn't need her parents in the classic sense. You might not need your parents to feed you, but it's nice to know that there's somebody out there who has known you always and loves you absolutely. When you have no parents, you don't have that sense.

I am envious of friends who have parents who come over and baby-sit, or give them money for a down payment on a house. I think those people have a security and solidity in their view of life that I don't have. I think of them as resting on a big mattress. And I'm floating on the ocean, all by myself.

I joke about wanting to put myself up for adoption. I'm kind of serious. I think, "There are all these nice old people out there. Maybe they had a child who died, or maybe they just have a kid who's bratty and ungrateful. I'm really nice. I turned out okay. I can supply nice grandchildren." I could start an adopt-an-older-child website. But then I think, well, they'd be calling all the time. Maybe they'd want to tell me what to do. What if they got sick and I had to go sit in the hospital? I think I'm used to this now.

LIFE BECAME POSSIBLE

I think that when both of your parents die when you're young, death is in the air. It seems more possible than life, in some ways. When I was forty-two I got an assignment from *Good Housekeeping* to write a story on the power of age—how being a certain age reverberates in your psyche and forms choices you make. I was thinking about these issues, and I suddenly realized that I was the age my mother was when she got sick. I became aware that I carried around an unconscious expectation that I, too, would get sick. I always assumed that I'd be crippled or dead by the age of fifty or sixty. I believed it, the way you believe your eyes are blue or something. Once I became conscious of that, it affected the way I thought about my life and my choices. I realized I had no real vision of what it was like to be a woman getting older. I didn't have images of women in their fifties and sixties and beyond being vital and loving and alive, so I started searching for an image of an older woman who might have a life I wanted to have.

I went to an artists' colony recently to work on a book, and there were several women in their sixties, some of whom had always been artists and some who had other careers first. I was fascinated by them. I think that my work is so central to my life because it is a way to make myself unlike my mother. I saw her as smart and energetic and driven, but she was also a frustrated housewife and an angry mother. I didn't want to be her in any way.

I carried around an unconscious expectation that I, too, would get sick.

Once I got over assuming I was going to die, and grasped that even if I did get sick, I still didn't have to die, then suddenly life became possible. I realized that I had the power to try to stay alive, to not vanish on my children. To stay engaged in their lives. To be a parent of children getting older, moving into adulthood, in a way that I didn't have.

For many years I was a smoker. After my father died and my last kid was born, my brother said, "Why are you still smoking? You're somebody who could actually have a good old age. You have nice children; your husband's from a family where everybody lives to be a hundred. And you're killing yourself." I threw out my cigarettes that day.

I think that unlike a lot of parents, I am conscious of how much parenting a child needs from the age of thirteen on. I put a tremendous amount of effort into connecting with my teenagers and trying to have a good relationship with my twenty-one-year-old daughter. I understand how much, even at twenty-one, she needs me, and I encourage her to need me. Because I missed that.

The whole idea of inventing my old age, and continuing my relationship with my kids as I get older, is a big one for me. I'm a bit obsessed with it. What will old age look like? What do I want it to look like? If I'm feeling optimistic, which maybe I am today, I look at the future as a great opportunity. I have the freedom to invent it. I'm not stuck on a track, because there is no track. I'm not stuck with an image of how to get old, or what getting old is, or what a grown-up relationship is like with parents, because I didn't have it. So I can create what I think it should be.

Yogi Berra

YOGI BERRA
They Died Too Young

I LEFT HOME WHEN I WAS seventeen years old. Now I'm eighty-one. Every time I go back to St. Louis, I think of my parents. My sister still lives in the house we grew up in. She is younger than I am; we're the only ones left. She saved a lot of family mementos. She changed the house a little, but when I go back inside, I still remember what it looked like then—what rooms there were, where I slept, and all that.

Every Christmas when my parents were alive, my wife and I always went home with the kids to St. Louis to visit both sides of the family. My wife's family is all from around there, too. After my parents died it wasn't the same. Now I get to see my friends when I go home, the guys I grew up with. Those guys were good to me—they kept me on the straight line. But it is sad that my parents are gone. My mom died too young, and I think my dad died a little too young, too.

My parents are buried side by side. I visit their gravesites when I go home.

YOU GOTTA PLAY, NO MATTER WHAT

My dad didn't know anything about baseball. He didn't know what baseball was. He wanted me to go to work so I could bring home a check. My parents got to know baseball better after I started playing ball in 1947. They thought my Most Valuable Player award was great. I kidded my dad, "If you'd let all your sons play ball, you'd be a millionaire." He said, "Blame your mother."

I was thirty-four when Mom died of diabetes. I was away; she died in May, during baseball season. I regret not being there. I tried to get my dad to come up and live with us when my mom passed away, but he wanted to stay up on the hill in St. Louis where all his friends were.

Dad died two years later, in 1961, from heart trouble. I was not with him when he died, either. I had gone to visit him in the hospital when I was playing in St. Louis. When he died, my brothers called me to come on home.

I remember Walter Cooper, the catcher for the Cardinals, playing when his father died. I don't think he even went to the funeral —he had to play. When a parent died, they wouldn't let us go home. When our wives had babies, they wouldn't let us go home. It wasn't considered manly. You gotta play, no matter what. It's a little different today—the players go home.

I regret not being there.

I was involved in baseball when my parents died, so it kind of makes you forget a little bit. You forget, you know; you actually do. You're concentrating so hard on playing the game. I think my dad would have liked that. Move along; life has to go on. This is the way life is: You must keep going.

I think you need to deal with your parent's death on your own.

MY KIDS, MY DEATH

It was a big thrill to be elected to the Hall of Fame in 1972. I felt bad that my parents weren't there. I was thinking of them at the moment I was inducted. I think every mother and father would love to see that.

I tell my kids stories about my parents. I tell them where they were born, how they came over to America.

When a parent died, they wouldn't let us go home.

My mother was very sensitive. My dad was pretty tough. They were good people.

My three boys are real good. We get along real good. How they prepare for my death would be up to them, I guess.

I don't know if I'll see my parents again when I die. I don't think about that. I'll see what happens when it happens. I'm just glad I get up in the morning.

Valerie Webb

VALERIE WEBB
The Two Lights Were My Parents

MY MOTHER DIED of a heart attack in 2000, when I was ten years old, and my father was killed in the World Trade Center attacks on September 11, 2001. Six months after that, I was asked to flip the switch for the Tribute in Light ceremony, when two beams rose up to the sky in the place of the buildings.

I sat onstage next to New York City Mayor Michael Bloomberg and the former mayor, Rudolph Giuliani, and looked out at hundreds of people and flashing cameras. I was nervous. Mayor Bloomberg said, "I understand where you're coming from. I lost my father, too." At the right moment I turned around and flipped the switch. Everybody was pointing up at the lights. When the ceremony was over, the organizer said, "You did such a good job. We're proud of you."

When I looked up at the lights, I thought about my father and my mother. I imagined that the two lights were my parents. It was really special. Later, when I went home to Jersey City, New Jersey, I could even see the lights from there.

IT SEEMED LIKE A BAD DREAM

My dad was a police officer for the Port Authority. He lived with us in Jersey City until I was four, and then he moved to Queens, and I stayed with my mother. She was a nurse. We lived on the top floor of a two-family house. I saw my father every weekend, and when I was in third grade, he started picking me up from school on Mondays, Wednesdays, and Fridays.

I liked living with my mom. She helped me with my homework, and we had fun together. I was her only child.

My mother was helping my aunt get her car inspected when she started complaining of chest pain. They went to the hospital and ran some tests; the doctor said everything was fine. But while she was at the hospital, she had a heart attack. I was home with my grandmother. The phone rang, and I answered. My aunt said, "Your mother just had a heart attack. Put Ma on the phone." So I gave the phone to my grandmother. We got dressed and went to the hospital and sat in the waiting room. Every now and then a doctor would come out and say, "We don't know how things are going. We don't know if she is going to make it."

Finally we got to see her. She was in a coma. I held her hand, but she didn't respond. Once in a while she moved, but it didn't matter if you said anything. I knew something was wrong, but I thought she was going to come out of it. She was young. I couldn't imagine that anything bad was going to happen.

The next day they ran more tests, and the doctors said that she was brain-dead. They told me that my mother wasn't going to make it. Until then, I had thought she would wake up. A couple of days later, they took her off life support. There was nothing they could do.

When it first happened, I was crying all the time, but after a while I didn't anymore. One of my best friends was there through it all. Every day she called me up. The day of my mother's wake, she called me, crying, and said, "Are you alright?" I wasn't even crying, and she was.

For a long time it seemed like a bad dream. At school there were all kinds of rumors. People called me up, saying, "I heard your mother was in a car accident." Somebody else said, "I heard you moved." After a while I realized it was real, and I adapted to not having a mom. I moved in with my grandmother. I got used to it, but I still miss my mother a lot. Other kids say, "My mom did this," or "My mom got me that." I can't say any of those things.

I was very close to my mom. I think about her a lot. When I look in the mirror, it reminds me of her. My eyes look like hers. Someday I want to get a tattoo of my mother's name. My grandmother says I can get one, but not yet. I have to be a little older.

SEPTEMBER 11

My father worked out of the Holland Tunnel. He was a traffic cop. He had to go to traffic court every Tuesday and Thursday. Those were the days he couldn't pick me up from school. On Monday, September 10, 2001, my father said, "I'll see you on Wednesday.

Call me tomorrow night to make sure I can pick you up." I said goodbye, and that was it.

The next morning I was in school, in first period, when a plane roared overhead. My school is in downtown Jersey City, minutes from New York. People were working on the side of our building, and my teacher left our class to see what was going on. "The work crews are going crazy," she said. "Something's happening outside." The teacher came back in and said, "Does anybody have parents up there in the World Trade Center?" Everybody said no.

We switched classes like normal. And then kids' parents started picking them up from school. I could see the smoke out the window and firefighters and ambulances going by. *I was in school, in first period, when a plane roared overhead.* I said, "When am I going to get picked up?" My friend, whose father was also a police officer, said, "Well, if my father's going to come pick me up, your father's going to come pick you up." But then they called me down to the office, and my aunt was there.

We went to my grandmother's house, and I called the Holland Tunnel to see where my father was. I thought he was in court, since it was a Tuesday. They said, "We can't give out any information because we don't know where anybody is right now." I called back and told them I was his daughter, and they said, "He was sent over to the World Trade Center, but we haven't heard from him. Call back in a couple of hours." I kept calling, and they didn't know anything. They said they couldn't get a radio signal. That night I went to bed thinking that my dad was probably working and just couldn't get to a phone. I thought, "He'll call tomorrow. He'll get my message and call me back."

One day went by, and then another. I called my dad's cell phone, and it kept going straight to voice mail. I thought, *Okay, maybe he turned his phone off.* So I left messages. I said, "Dad, if you get this, call me back. I want to know what's going on." I thought he might be in the hospital.

I kept hoping. I kept calling the Holland Tunnel, and they still didn't tell me anything. All of my family was there, though, so it didn't seem like such a big deal. I thought I'd hear from him that day or the next. At one point when I called, they told me that somebody said they had seen him. But I found out later that it was the wrong cop.

I didn't go back to school the next week, so people wondered where I was. When I finally went back to school, everyone knew what had happened. So a lot of people were there for me. The next month in school, they had a tribute to the victims of 9/11. The mayor of Jersey City came and awarded plaques to me and another girl who had lost her father. Now in my school there is a wall dedicated to police officers and civilians who died on 9/11.

THEY NEVER FOUND HIS BODY

When my mother died, I had my father. My father's death was a different kind of loss. I got to see my mother when she was sick. But I saw my father the day before he died, and that was it. Every day there was a news report like, "We found two cops, and they haven't been identified yet." We would think it was his body, but it never was. It was hard not knowing. They never found his body. They didn't find a badge or a hat, or anything that belonged to him. The only way we know he went to the World Trade Center is because all cops were dispatched, and he never came back.

That November, our family held a memorial service. When a police officer dies, the Port Authority gives the family a new uniform with gloves and a shirt, so I have those things to remember him by.

My grandma helped me get through the grief. I could talk to her and feel better.

My family and friends also helped. They take my mind off things; I can have fun with them, which makes it easier.

I think it's important not to shut yourself off. And not to think that you're the only one. There are camps for relatives of 9/11 victims, and I go every summer. Most of the kids who go there haven't lost both of their parents, but a lot have lost their fathers. We all know where we're coming from. We're all close. I have made a lot of good friends there.

I don't think my parents would have wanted me to be sad all the time.

PROUD OF ME

I wish I had at least one parent. People are surprised that I don't have either. When other kids find out you've lost both parents, they look at you differently. Most of the time they don't keep questioning. If people ask, I'll tell them what happened, but I don't tell them everything. I just say my parents are deceased.

If my parents were here, my life would be different. I think about them a lot. I might be writing something for school and suddenly it will remind me of a time my mother helped me. Or I could be just sitting, doing my homework, and I'll remember something about my dad. I remember the cologne my father wore. If I get close to someone who smells like that, it reminds me of him.

I know where my mother is buried. I haven't gone there yet. I don't like cemeteries. On my mother's birthday there is usually a mass at church, and I go there. I have my mother's bed and chairs and other furniture, and they remind me of good times. They remind me of her.

My father always told me, "Anything you want, you can have." My mother would say, "Don't tell her that!" Every weekend my father and I went to Toys "R" Us and bought Barbie dolls and clothes. My mother would say, "Where are you going to put all this stuff?" I have a necklace *I don't think my parents would have wanted me to be sad all the time.* my father gave me, a heart that says "I love you." I wear it a lot. When I wear the things he gave me, I feel closer to him. I also have a dog that he bought me named Kane.

When September 11 is talked about on the news, it reminds me of the day I lost my father. But it doesn't really bother me. I understand that what happened was a tragedy, but mainly I think about the fact that my father died as a hero.

The day of the Tribute in Light ceremony, I left school early and went home. A car later picked us up to take us to New York. I went up onstage, and when it was time, I flipped the switch. When I got home, people were calling the house, saying, "I saw Valerie on TV!" A few months later, a girl came up to me and said she had seen me in *JET* magazine. After a while I just wanted to go back to being regular old Valerie. But one day outside of school, a guy was looking at me, and finally he said, "Weren't you the girl who lit the light?" I said I was. He said, "I just wanted to say I saw you on TV. I'm proud of you."

I think my parents would have been proud of me, too.

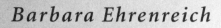

Barbara Ehrenreich

BARBARA EHRENREICH
My Father Didn't Recognize Me

I ALWAYS HAD a better relationship with my dad than I did with my mother. We had a certain kind of connection. In many ways, he was very supportive of me. My father started out in poverty as a copper miner in Butte, Montana, a brawling, roughneck, violent place. He managed to get some education by going to school and studying metallurgy while he was a miner. Then he rocketed into the middle class, even ending up in the upper middle class. He was a paradoxical figure: sarcastic and funny, extremely kind and extremely cruel. Which person was he? I don't know; I never figured it out.

I was brought up by both my parents to respect everybody's work. They had both done hard work. While my father valued education, at some level he looked down on people who only had that. I was supposed to succeed and get an education, but then he'd tell me my professors were full of shit, that if they really knew anything, they'd do it, they wouldn't teach it.

My father *saw* people. He saw everybody. If he was in a hotel, you'd find him chatting with the hotel housekeeper. I remember being with him in New York City when I was in my twenties, and coming across a bum lying on the sidewalk. My father stopped and crouched down by the person, helping him. He stayed there until a cop came.

When my father first started showing symptoms of Alzheimer's disease, I went out to California to help. He began to be unable to care for himself. It didn't look like a good situation, and I was really worried.

Ultimately, he ended up in a facility for people with Alzheimer's in Denver, which is where my sister lives. My brother and sister and I had long talks in trying to deal with my father's illness. I would go out about every month from Long Island and spend two or three days with him. It was time-consuming and totally depressing. My father was a brilliant man; he was a genius in science. It was a very big part of his identity. He was smarter than anybody else in the world. And now he couldn't really talk.

When I visited, we would go to one of those god-awful restaurants that are all pies. Once I tried to take him to a matinee, but he hated that. A lot of people with Alzheimer's find too much stimulation overwhelming. So we'd basically just go out and eat and drive around. When the weather was decent, I'd try to get him to walk, which he hated. I felt both an obligation and a real attachment to him, which made it more painful.

Alzheimer's is creepy. To lose somebody while they're still physically present is like having somebody stuffed and sitting around in your living room. It's the same face, roughly speaking, but the person you love is not behind it.

At a certain point, my father didn't recognize me. The last time I saw him alive, I had gone out there with my daughter, Rosa, who was in college. He was much taken with Rosa; she is a prettier version of me. He got out something coherent, which was that I was getting fat. (I think that was a bit of an exaggeration!) He would only pay attention to Rosa. I think he actually thought she was just the new, updated version of me—the upgraded version.

I was not with my father when he died; I got a phone call. My husband and I were having people over for a picnic in the backyard. And I remember thinking, "Well, I'm just going to go on with this picnic." In a way, he'd been dead for quite a while for me.

To lose somebody while they're still physically present is like having somebody stuffed and sitting around in your living room.

But then I began to notice, as the day went on, that I was numb. I couldn't interact with other people. I wasn't really there with them. I couldn't just push it away like that; I couldn't just chit-chat with people.

I did not go back to Denver. It was very different from my response to my mother's death, when all I could think was, *Oh my god, I've got to get there. I've got to be with my sister, my brother, my aunt.* With my father, it was just like—*Ugh, well, that's over.* When my mother died, I had lots of relatives asking me to come for a service. There was no such thing after my father died. He had left behind his friends a long time ago. It was his children, period.

It did not enter my mind to feel a sense of orphanhood when my father died. There are two deaths with Alzheimer's: There's when they actually die and get cremated or buried, and there's the death before that.

We donated my father's brain for Alzheimer's research and had him cremated. Within the year, my brother and sister and I came together and had a memorial service among ourselves. My husband and two of my brother's children were there, too. We put my father's ashes in a really stupid lake. I can't describe it any other way—I just thought it was a completely inadequate lake. It was on the Arkansas-Missouri border, and we got on a little pontoon boat with the ashes. I had not grieved until that point. What are you going to say—"He had Alzheimer's. Thank God it's over"? You know? He's gone. And then when we got out there on the lake, everything was wrong. The lake was murky. The hills were too low. My father came from the mountains. That was when it hit. And I just started to sob. I felt very protective, like he deserved a better lake.

AN ELEMENT OF MYSTERY

Years earlier, when I was thirty-five, I learned from my aunt that my mother had died. It was a terrible phone call. My aunt was very mad at me; she was yelling at me, saying that I had been unreachable. I was living in New York, as a graduate student in biology, and had been traveling. This was before answering machines or cell phones.

That was, I think, my aunt's way of dealing with her own anger, and maybe even some sense of guilt. I was quite taken aback—as much by that as by the news itself. I loved this aunt, too. I don't think she blamed me directly, but that was the message.

My mother was fifty-four when she died, and there is an element of mystery to her death. It appears to have been suicide. She didn't leave a note.

I don't know if she would have been classified as depressed, but she was generally a very unhappy person; she had an unhappy marriage and an unhappy divorce.

I was stunned. My mother's death was out of the blue. My mother and father had been divorced for twelve or fourteen years, she had remarried, and superficially things seemed to be alright. I don't know if they were. Possibly she was having some trouble in that marriage; I don't know. But I had figured things were better. I didn't know how to process it. I had to arrange to fly out to Iowa, where my mother had been living. My children were about five and three at the time, and I didn't take them with me. I don't think I could have afforded it, for one thing. We had a memorial service in Ames, Iowa, and I was chosen by my brother and sister to give a little talk. I busied myself doing that, and I didn't really grieve.

When my mother died, I felt a lot of sadness about her whole life, about her own sadness and anger. I knew she died too early. She was too young. She was a very energetic, intelligent person who didn't have anything to do with all that energy and intelligence. Her life was [out of Betty Friedan's] *The Feminine Mystique*. At the funeral I talked about how, looking back at my mother's life, I think there was an anger about how she had been a misfit and hadn't fit into the fifties-era ideal of marvelous womanhood. She wanted more, but didn't know how to define that. Then she moved to Iowa as a divorced woman. It was very difficult for her to integrate into the community as a divorcée. She had never been accepted much into the community.

So there was a certain edge to my talk. I was saying that she had been too large, in some ways, for the circumstances she was given. I felt very involved in the talk, and I felt like I was trying to sort of speak for her.

Like many women of my generation, I had a great determination not to end up in that kind of situation, where I would be financially dependent on a man, with no outlets for creativity other than domestic things. I was one in the generation of younger women who said, "I'm not going down that path."

My relationship with my mother when I was growing up was difficult. We were not close. Once I was out of the house, she wasn't a regular presence in my life. I didn't get in touch with her as often as I should have, and she didn't call and chat. My mother was not very involved with any of her children, and she was not very involved in my children's lives as a grandmother. I remember once, she came to New York with her second husband and didn't even tell me she had come—and I had two small children then. That's indicative of how she was.

When you have a relationship that has so much ambivalence in it, you know that it's not going to get resolved, and I don't think it would have been resolved if she had continued to live.

My mother died in August, and for years, my sister would say August was a rough time of year for her. But I never felt that. I think one's parents—perhaps especially your mother, if you're a woman—actually live in you. For example, my mother taught me everything I know about heavy-duty housecleaning. I can't even distinguish her voice from my mine when I'm cleaning. The voice will be saying, "Wait a minute, that's lazy. Move that chair. Don't just go around it—you've got to move it." Or I'll be with my granddaughter, who just turned four. We'll be cooking something, and I'll say, "I learned to do this from my mommy. She always did this and that." A lot of my connection with my mother is at this level of manual labor, a physical relationship to the world.

THE FRONT OF THE LINE

My parents didn't have a lot—there was no money or property to be concerned with—but they had books. Those books were precious to me when I was a child. I wish that some of the books had survived, but they didn't make it through the many moves.

After my mother died, I kept a beautiful brooch that she had gotten from her grandmother. I treasured it. The brooch was an unusual kind of enamel, a little picture of a seagull on a silver pin. It was very pretty. It was made in the nineteenth century, in Canada, where my mother was from. But when we lived in Syosset, Long

Island, somebody broke into the house and took all my jewelry, most of which was just cheap crap. But they also took the brooch. I felt bad about it; it was the only piece I had of hers. But what does it tell you about her? Nothing. Maybe because I am a writer, I think that the stories are more important, anyway. So it's the anecdotes about things that I really treasure, the cooking and cleaning, that I will pass on to my own children.

There's no physical place where my parents are. But I don't feel any need to have a place to go. They are in me, insofar as they continue. My sister and I talked a lot about the deaths of our parents. I think that is very important.

I always imagine that we're in a queue, a long queue heading for the edge of a cliff. And the queue just moves ahead.

But each sibling experiences a different parent, in a way, even when you're talking about one person. My sister's version of my mother is very different from mine. My brother's version of our father is very different from mine. But these are the people who share memories with you. Talking to my siblings helps me to look at things in my own mind, to understand better what my parents were all about, to draw a lesson.

I was very close to the aunt who yelled at me after my mother died. So when this aunt died, it was very painful. I remember having conversations with my cousins, her daughters, about how we had to keep the family together now. This aunt had done so much to keep us together. We decided to get together when we can. We look for ways to get together, because we're geographically scattered. Phone calls and emails—the usual things. It feels like something you have to grow up and realize—you know, Aunt Jean isn't there keeping track of people's birthdays anymore. And nobody's going to do it unless you do it.

I don't feel protective or secretive about my experience of loss. I always imagine that we're in a queue, a long queue heading for the edge of a cliff. And the queue just moves ahead. Some people fall over the edge, and you just go on. That's how it seems to me. I can't think of too many people ahead of me; I have one aunt now who is of the earlier generation. Otherwise, I'm getting toward the front of the line.

Sergeant Michael Treanor

SERGEANT MICHAEL TREANOR
If I Could Have One Thing...

AT THE AGE OF THIRTY-ONE, I had a wife and children and thought I was pretty well-prepared for anything. Then I lost my parents and realized I didn't know as much as I thought. I was an orphan and never felt more lost and alone.

Losing both of your parents at the same time is extremely hard. When you lose one, you can always fall back on the other. But when you lose both, you have nobody. You don't recover completely; there's a line drawn in your life between before and after. You never get over it—you just find a way to deal with it. Nobody will ever replace your mom and dad.

I like to think of myself as a happy person today, but if I could have one thing in the world, it would be to have them back.

NEVER COMING HOME

The morning of the Oklahoma City bombing, April 19, 1995, I was at work in a small farming community about thirty-five miles north of the city. I worked in a metal shop next to a train track, so when I heard a loud rumble, I thought an engineer had slammed some cars together too hard. It turned out to be the shock wave from the blast. I didn't think much more of it until about forty-five minutes later, when one of the guys who worked in the shop came up to me and said, "I hear they're activating us." We were both in the National Guard. He said that a building had been bombed in Oklahoma City. I thought he was pulling a prank. Then I learned from the supervisors in the office, who had a radio, that it was the Federal Building, and the damage was severe.

I had seen my parents the night before. I was picking up my kids; my parents had watched them every day for ten years. That night, I told them I loved them and said goodbye. It turned out my father had a 9:00 AM appointment to get his social security worked out, and my mother went along and brought Ashley, my wife's four-year-old daughter from her first marriage, to keep him company. My parents spent as much time together as possible; they were probably the most in love couple I've ever met.

That night, we drove up to my parents' house. Seeing it dark and still, we knew they were never coming home.

At about 11:30 AM, my brother called to ask if I'd heard from them. I said no. My brother told me that my dad had the day off, and I knew he had had to go to the social security office. I began to get real nervous. I met my wife, Kathleen, at the hospital, where victims' names were beginning to be posted. She was in tears, but

I was trying to stay calm and focused. When officials would go to the board and write down names of people they'd found, and Ashley's and my parents' names weren't there, Kathleen would just fall apart. She was overwhelmed by not knowing what happened to them.

The hospital was getting swamped with the crowds, so they set up a family-assistance center nearby with grief counselors. Kathleen and I went there. My sister went to my parents' house to see if they were home, and my brother went from one Red Cross center to another in search of information. That night, we drove up to my parents' house. Seeing it dark and still, we knew they were never coming home. It was a complete sense of panic, like being lost in the woods at night.

We weren't officially notified of what happened to my parents and Ashley for four or five days. During that time my family needed me to be strong for them, so I focused on their needs, not mine. That probably helped me deal with it.

All three bodies were found close to each other near the front of the building, sixty feet from the epicenter of the blast. My dad's body was intact, though he had burns on his face from the explosion. My mom was crushed; there was no way we could view her body. Ashley was found near my parents. The medical examiner and the funeral parlor director strongly advised us not to view her body. She was pretty bad; they told us her back and the back of her skull were smashed and missing. Ashley's father insisted on seeing her, though. He needed to verify, for himself, that it was really her.

REVENGE

I don't know anybody else who has lost both of their parents at once like that. There were days I didn't know if I could go on. I really wanted Timothy McVeigh put to death. I imagined exacting my revenge on him and anyone else who had been involved in the bombing. I went through a period when I was uncomfortable being in church because of what I was thinking. Being in the military, I knew I was better prepared to seek revenge on the guy who did this than most people. But I knew that would make me no better than he was. Revenge was not what Jesus taught.

I was uncomfortable being in church because of what I was thinking.

It helps to accept that whatever it was that took your parents from you, it was out of your control. A lot of people beat themselves up. You can't do that. When McVeigh was executed, it was so long after the bombing that I was pretty well-recovered, but I did feel he finally got what he deserved. I did get some satisfaction from that.

We still have my parents' house, but no one lives there. My parents lived across a wooded creek from me, and the house is still full of their belongings. For a long time, we kept the contents close to the way they were the day my parents died, but recently we've begun to remodel it so, one day, my brother, who now owns it, can have the choice to move back in. My father never did a will; he couldn't decide how to divide things up between the kids, and he always thought he had lots of time. This lack of guidance made things very difficult.

At first my sister was reluctant to move on. To her, dividing up our parents' belongings and dealing with their estate meant they were really gone, and she was not ready for that. But certain things had to get done. Dad had some land and owned 250 head of cattle. We had to decide what to do with them. The farm needed attention that night—the night of the bombing. The farm is a living, breathing thing that couldn't be ignored. Crops are growing; cattle need to be fed. Now, all of a sudden, there was a farm to run—and none of us was ready for that responsibility. My sister was too grief-stricken. My two younger brothers had their own opinions of how to handle things. I could hardly make a move without it being wrong. We eventually pulled together, but it was intense while it was happening. I wouldn't want to do it again.

EVERY MOMENT IS PRECIOUS

My life is more defined by my parents' lives than by their deaths. They were honest people and never lied to anyone. They were able to make business deals with handshakes, and they taught me to be the same way. People count on me, and I try never to disappoint them. I think work is important and you have to go, even when you're not feeling up to it. I'd have to be on my knees to call in sick to work. I never want to do anything to shame my family or my parents' memories.

I share stories of my parents with my children, especially at the holidays. It's important to keep their memories alive. They were parents, counselors, neighbors, daycare for my family, everything.

While I think about my parents every day, I try not to focus on how they were taken from me. But if a violent explosion makes the news, I quickly flash back to how they died. If something is mentioned specifically about the bombing or there's an anniversary of the event, I can't help but be reminded. The Oklahoma City National Memorial is a nice way to remember them, although I don't find much comfort there. I find comfort where I live—and where they used to live—at the farm. That's where the pleasant memories are. I did a lot of handyman work for them around the house. I built my mother a new porch. It was the last thing I did for them.

I do think I'll see my parents again. I'm sure of it. It's incredible how much my family and I relied on religion after my parents died. It carried us through the worst of it.

I regret that I didn't spend more time with my parents when they were alive. We were all so preoccupied—I was busy with my job, my National Guard duty, my family. As a teenager, you think you know it all, and you don't want anything to do with your parents. But as you get older, you realize their wisdom. When I became a father, I began to rely on them for advice on raising my children. I realized after my parents were gone that many opportunities were missed.

I don't look for temporary Guard duty out of state anymore; I have learned that every moment is precious.

Shelby Lynne

SHELBY LYNNE
I'm Not One of the Victims

SOMETIMES I FEEL I've lived a very long life, because a lot has happened in the thirty-seven years I have been alive. I feel like an old person most of the time, but I don't feel bad about it. I would not have the life I have now if my parents were alive. Since the day they died, I've always done exactly what I want to do, when I want to do it, how I want to do it. I'm my own woman. That was all the jet fuel I needed to propel me in life.

Having dead parents gave me room to focus on myself. I think one of the reasons I'm successful is that what I love to do is music, and that's all I had. I never write songs about what happened to my parents. As an artist, though, I think you draw from pain, and what happened was definitely very painful. But life goes on; you have your scars and your battle wounds, and you just keep going.

As an artist, I think you draw from pain.

I'll never forget the date my parents died. It'll be twenty years this year, and I still hate the day.

TWO GUNSHOTS, TWO FUNERALS

It was five o'clock in the morning on a Tuesday. I was seventeen years old, my parents were separated, and I was at my mother's house in Mobile, Alabama. My dad pulled up to the house, and Mom had just put on a pot of coffee. They went outside to talk. I heard two gunshots; he shot and killed her, and then he killed himself. I walked outside and found them dead.

A friend of my mother's was staying there that night with us, and we called the police. They asked me what happened and I told them, and they left. I called all of our family and told them. Two days later we had two funerals, one for my mother and one for my father. We buried them in two different places on the same day.

There you have it. That's the end of it.

My parents are buried out in the woods somewhere in Alabama. I never visit their gravesites. I never understood doing that; I think it's silly to put a plaque in the dirt.

After our parents died, my younger sister, Allison, and I went to live with my mother's sister and her family. It wasn't really a family home. There were a lot of homes involved, a lot of moving around and separating. After my sister and I finished high school, we began to live two separate lives. She went to college, and I got married and went to record records.

My relationship with Allison has definitely improved through the years. Sometimes we haven't been that close. Now, we talk about our lives; we respect each other and love each other unconditionally. The older we get, the closer we get. We know that we have each other, period. There's no other human being on earth who understands what happened that day and understands who we are as people. Life is a privilege—it's so easy to die. That's a survivor's way of life. And we've always understood that.

Allison lives in New York. We don't get to see each other a lot, but we write letters and talk on the phone. We'd love to see each other more, but it's not pressing. We're not needy creatures. We love who we love and keep them close. No matter how many miles away, or what comes between us, or who I'm with, or who she's with, that won't change. Even in death, we'll have each other. We have a bond that's unbreakable.

We don't have any of our parents' stuff. There was so much moving around, and through the years things get shuffled around and lost. I have a couple of pictures, but they don't mean anything. Looking at the pictures of my parents is like looking at strangers. It was so long ago. The older you get and the longer it's been, you start seeing them the way their pictures look. You're looking at a photograph and you think, *Did they really look like that?* It seems like a life that isn't mine—that's so far away. I don't recognize any of it. Those pictures got nothing to do with my life anymore.

IT TAKES OVER

When you're in the entertainment business, you're in the public. And they want to know everything there is to know about you. The more horrible it is, the happier they are. That's just the fact. There's no escaping it, and you can't control it. That's why I never bring up what happened. It's something I just don't talk about.

Journalists basically write what they want to write, no matter what you say. I always say, "Let's talk about the music. This is about my album, not my dead parents." And they usually respect it, as far as not bringing it up to me in an interview.

Am I lucky or unlucky? I think I'm both. But I choose to look at the lucky.

But they're going to write about it anyway. I've turned down a lot of press in the last few years for that reason. It takes over. It takes the focus off everything else. I can make the record of my career, and my dead parents take front and center every time. So, it's a burden.

It's also been embarrassing sometimes in my life to have this situation with Mom and Daddy. If it comes up at a party or in conversation, nobody can concentrate on anything else. It was a traumatic, unusual thing. A lot of people have dead parents, but you don't hear about murder-suicides every day.

SETTING ME FREE

I think that you have to be careful when you have dead parents, and they've been gone for so long, that you don't make them out to be more than they were. It'd be easy for me to make my father a hero and my mother look like a queen. I'm careful consciously not to say, "I had the greatest parents." *No, you didn't*, I tell myself. *If you had the greatest parents in the world,*

they wouldn't be six feet under, you know? They didn't have it together. I refuse to make heroes out of people who pretty much
ruined my life. And I won't give them *that* credit, even. They
didn't ruin my life. I think I've done pretty damn well. And
dead parents or not, here I am.

People don't believe it, but I was relieved—and still am—
that I didn't have to take care of my parents anymore. I took
care of them as a kid, and they were a pain. I carried a lot of
weight around for seventeen years, and I didn't deserve it. So it
was good for me to let them to go, and I'm still glad they're gone.
That was their way of setting me free.

Most people have the burden of having to take care of older
or sickly parents. Am I lucky or unlucky? I think I'm both. But I
choose to look at the lucky.

KICK ASS AND BECOME SOMETHING

I know what it feels like to have the rug snatched from under me,
and not just Mom and Daddy's deaths—many experiences in my
life. The difference is that I'm aware of it, and grateful for it. I'm not
saying I've got the market sewn up on knowing what life's about.
But I feel like I know what's important. And I know that I'm fortunate to know.

My advice to people is don't be stuck. You can sit around and
cry all day, or you can go kick ass and become something. In order
to get through life, in my opinion, you have to face it head-on. I'm
not afraid of that. I try to keep going forward.

When I was younger, I did a lot of crying, a lot of breaking things, a lot of, "Oh, look what the world has done to me." It doesn't work. The world hasn't done anything to you. This is the life you were born to live, and you do the best with it that you can. Pick and choose your partners and your friends carefully. I feel like I have; I can count them on two hands. How lucky is that?

I never had the need to go talk with someone professionally about what happened. I feel safe enough to talk about it with people who love me. Therapy is for the birds. I don't believe in it. I think it's a great way for people to make money.

People would love for me to be in therapy because of what happened. They say, "You're so angry." No, I'm not. I've moved on. I'm a strong individual. I don't like victims; I would never have chosen to be one. And I refuse to be around anybody who is. A lot of it for me is patience. I don't have any. People generally frustrate me. I feel like I've been there, done that. I don't let a lot of people in, because I don't want to deal with old bullshit that I've already dealt with twenty years ago. I also feel deeply. And I don't have a lot of patience for people who don't. I don't have patience for people who skip through life and nothing happens to them.

I don't mind facing life alone. I will never have children. And I will never be married again. Because in the end, what are you left with? You really can't depend on anybody or anything. You have to face God or yourself—and the world you've created for yourself in which to live. I think life is about not being afraid of what might happen next, knowing there is no control whatsoever about any of it. I'm not scared of anything. I never have been. Fear is a barrier between you and life. You can't be scared; you just have to live.

What happened with my parents is not holding me down. It doesn't make me angry; I simply let them go the day they chose to leave. The main story for me now is that I've left a life behind that didn't work out, and I'm doing just fine.

I'm not one of the victims.

Brian O'Hara

BRIAN O'HARA
Sleeping in Their Bed

IT WAS THE SUMMER after my seventh-grade year, and I was twelve years old. My parents and sister were heading to Paris for a few weeks for the Tour de France. My dad was executive producer of ABC Sports; he was going to cover the race. My sister, Caity, had taken French classes in school and was interested in going, but it was the last thing my twin brother, Matt, and I wanted to do. We had plans to attend basketball camp that week and stay with my grandparents.

When you're a kid, it's kind of a break when your parents leave. That's why it was so fun going to basketball camp. You're with a bunch of other kids, and there are no parents around. Matt and I were always on the same team and played the same sports. We were very competitive, as well—there was some sibling rivalry.

The last time I saw my mother, I was swimming at the country-club pool. She came to say goodbye. That's the only part of the day that I remember.

That night, around ten o'clock, I was in bed doing a crossword puzzle, listening to a sports radio station, and the announcer said that a plane had crashed going from New York to Paris. I felt little butterflies in my stomach, but I thought, *No way—my parents flew on an earlier flight.* My grandfather came into my room all flustered and asked where my mom's telephone book was. I said, "What's going on?" A few moments later I went downstairs, and my grandparents were watching TV and were very upset.

I didn't know what to think. My uncle came over, and then more people, eight or ten altogether, came to the house. We were all in the kitchen, watching TV. At first I was in shock, dumbfounded and upset. It was about a half hour until we knew for sure. My grandfather called the airline to confirm the flight. Once we verified that it was TWA flight 800, I lost control for a couple of hours.

At about midnight I went outside to shoot a basketball, just to get out of the house. Then I went to sleep in my parents' bed. I rarely did that. You'd think that it would be weird—my parents are dead, and I'm sleeping in their bed. But it wasn't. It felt right.

The next day the house was crowded with people making phone calls all day, making the necessary arrangements. Even though they said there were no survivors, I was hoping there were. I kept expecting to turn on the TV again and see the good news. In my mind, I had a picture of people in a life raft in the middle of the ocean. Even a week afterward, when I was watching the news and they said something about survivors, I turned the volume up, thinking,

Oh my god, maybe there is somebody—not realizing that there's no chance of being in the Atlantic Ocean for a week. So it didn't really hit me until several weeks later, when I realized, *Wow—they're really not coming back.*

My parents had been very involved in the community; my mother was in the PTA and my dad coached our teams, basketball and baseball. For the funeral, TV screens were set up at the high school, like theaters, so people who couldn't get into the church could see it. It was nice to see how many people showed up—it felt good that there were so many people there.

I don't think more about my parents on the anniversary of their deaths. It's not something you want to think about every year.

But I also felt anxious because my brother and I were the focal point. You're a twelve-year-old kid, and all of a sudden hundreds of people are surrounding you and staring at you and thinking, *There's the kid who lost his family.*

My sister got lost in the mix. People would say, "Oh, your parents died," not "Oh, your parents and your sister died." She didn't have time to make an impact like my parents did. She was my big sister, and I had a great relationship with her; I think about her a lot.

My grandparents lived in our house for the summer. It was their idea to keep our lives as normal as possible. They didn't make huge changes to our schedule. My brother and I still went to basketball camp. It was weird—you lose your parents, then all of a sudden you're with a bunch of strangers playing basketball. No one knows your situation except for the supervisor and the coach. But it was also refreshing. The other kids didn't know; I was just another regular kid.

Once September rolled around, our grandparents went back to their home in Scarsdale. The last thing seventy-year-old people want is two twelve-year-olds running around. They couldn't keep up with us.

Our guardians were supposed to be my mom's brother and his wife. But they lived down in Philadelphia, and we wanted to stay near our friends in New York. My father's brother and his wife lived in Rockland County, only minutes from Irvington, and they moved into our house so we could finish eighth grade at our school.

It was weird to go from living with your parents, who know everything about you, to living with people you don't know very well. We didn't have a huge connection with them. It was strange to walk down the hallway and look in my parents' bedroom and see those people there. But it was also nice to know that they would screw up their entire lives to come and live with us so we could finish middle school in the same place.

They had a daughter who moved in, too. She stayed in my sister's room. It was crazy—you've got these three new people replacing the people who died. But it would have been a lot crazier if all of a sudden we'd had to pick up and move somewhere else. I was still in my own environment, in my own house. I still had the same friends.

When I went back to school, everyone knew my situation. I had seen a lot of my friends over the summer, and they were all at the funeral. But they can't know what it feels like unless it happens to them. People say, "I know what you're going through," but no one really understands, even if their parents have died. Every case is different. No one really knows what you're going through except you.

YOU THINK OF YOUR PARENTS EVERY DAY

For a while I think I was in shock. Then I got angry. I was angry to begin with; when I was little I had a short temper. But this definitely didn't help. I don't know if I expressed it outwardly, but I felt it inwardly. I'd think, *Why me?*

When your parents die, you also feel guilty over all those bad things you did when you were a kid, like talking back to your mom or fighting with your brother and upsetting your parents. But after a while you realize you can't go back and change it, so what's the point of feeling guilty? They made me go to a psychiatrist. He would ask me these questions, but I didn't really want to talk to anybody. I had a problem with authority—I didn't want to clean my room, much less go see a psychiatrist on a Monday night.

I didn't spend time blaming the government or the U.S. Navy, or anything else. The theories were far-fetched, and none of them were proven. If my parents had been murdered and one person were responsible, it might have been easier. But if some electrical engineering thing happened, you can't really blame the mechanic or the pilot. There's no one to blame. There was some kind of monetary compensation. But it can't bring my parents back. The airline could send a fruit basket, but there's not much else it could do.

My aunt and uncle always planned something on the anniversary of my parents' deaths. The first year or two, we went away, just to get out of the house. We didn't want to sit around doing nothing, twiddling our thumbs. One year we went down to Baltimore, and one year we went to Mystic Seaport.

On the five-year anniversary of the crash, we went to a big service at the end of Long Island, where they were dedicating a memorial to the victims. There was some candle-lighting. I didn't want to go. I'd rather have been outside swimming or playing golf than wasting a day sitting around with all these people in prayer. I thought it was stupid—all these families lined up with their candles. I felt obligated to go because my family was going. But I definitely didn't want to. Going to the ceremony was like watching the event itself unfold on the news; it didn't seem personal to me. I just saw the news coverage as a national event. I didn't feel like I was part of it.

You're scared of death at some point. And then at some point, you're motivated by it. You try to be more motivated than scared.

I don't think more about my parents on the anniversary of their deaths. Last year I didn't even realize it was the day until that afternoon. It's not something you want to think about every year.

Recently, I went to my parents' gravesite. It's not something that I love doing, but once a year it's nice to go there. It's definitely not healing for me, though. I don't have to be at the gravesite to think about them; you think of your parents every day. You run into days when all of a sudden it hits you, and it's even harder. Something might happen that makes you think about them, but it also might be for no good reason. There are all these times when you want your parents to be there, especially when you're growing up, going through high school, and all those important milestones. You want your parents to be around—to mold you, so to speak. But it isn't any harder on specific days.

One of the hardest times, though, is when a stranger asks you questions. I don't bring it up. I usually try to hide it; I don't want to go into the whole thing, especially with people I'm only going to talk to once.

I NEEDED TO SEE SOMEBODY

I am twenty-two years old now, and about a year ago I started seeing a psychiatrist. I had just graduated from college and needed to find a job and an apartment. I wasn't forced to go; I went on my own. I was ready. The psychiatrist told me that his father died, and it didn't really hit him until seven or eight years later. All of a sudden he was driving his car and it really hit him. I think it happened to me like that.

It boiled over ten years down the road. While I was studying abroad, my best friend died of a heart attack. Everything hit me at once. It brought back all these thoughts about my parents, that you could die at any moment. I started having anxiety attacks. I even went to a cardiologist—I thought, *Oh my god, maybe I'll have a heart attack.* I thought about it every day and was freaking out all the time. I really needed to see somebody.

Things have gotten better with time, and I've gotten my nerves under control. I can control my thoughts and put everything in perspective. Now, I try and think, *Okay, I could die any second—let me do something useful and worthwhile instead of fixating on my friend's death and my parents' deaths.* The last thing you want to do is walk around being timid your entire life, because how fun would that be? It's a waste. You're scared of death at some point. And then at some point you're motivated by it. You try, hopefully, to be more motivated than scared.

If you keep busy, you don't really have time to think about your parents' being gone. When it's the worst is when you have time to think, and you're just kind of sitting there, in your own thoughts and inside your own head. You have to run around and do things.

After you lose your parents, especially when you're a young kid, it can only get better. I mean, what else could happen to you? The next worst thing is for you to die yourself. What helps me most is thinking that even though I've been put in this adverse situation, I'm a stronger person for it—a better person. I definitely think I'm able to be a better friend. I can deal with a lot more than people who have had the comforts of their parents and not gone through tragedy.

JUST AS GOOD AS HE WAS

My grandparents kept a lot of my dad's clothes because they thought my brother and I would want them. I don't know what they were thinking—they're nice, but you don't want to wear your dead father's suits. I do have a lot of my father's ties. I wear them. Some are out of date, but I don't care. I've heard that paisley is coming back.

The artist Peter Max was a friend of my father's, and he painted several portraits of him. It's odd to have a picture of your dad up on the wall, especially when your friends come over. It's like your father is staring at you. It's weird, but it's also nice, and I love it.

I love to look at pictures of my parents. I was so young that a lot of the stuff I don't remember, and it doesn't even feel like I was there. But it's fun to see what you and your parents looked like when you—and they—were younger.

After my parents died, a combination of people—including my uncle and grandparents, our friends and the community—founded an annual basketball tournament in my parents' and sister's name for seventh- and eighth-grade boys and girls. It raises money for a number of local charities. For the first couple of years, it was weird to go to the event, because I was that kid whose parents had died. I always felt like everyone was looking at me. It wasn't a place I wanted to be. But as I've gotten older, it's something that I really enjoy. People come because they've been friends of the family for a long time. It's nice to see people in the sports world, friends of my father, help out. Celebrities also lend a hand and help us raise money. So it's been great, and it makes me proud.

I work for ABC now. A lot of the guys who work there were in the office when I was a little kid. Now I'm working for them. They take me under their wing and show me the ropes. I want to do well and be successful there. It feels good to be around these guys my father knew. I want to prove to them that I'm a smart kid who works hard—that I'm just as good as he was.

Even though my parents died when I was young, I still am who I am because of them. My brother and I never really talked about our parents' deaths—and still don't. We both know what happened. We can think about how our parents died and focus on that, or we can try and do something with our own lives. I don't want to sit around and feel sorry for myself.

Time is of the essence.

Catheryne Ilkovic Morgan

CATHERYNE ILKOVIC MORGAN
It Is My Duty to Remember Them

MY DAY STARTS WITH a prayer for my parents, who were killed in Auschwitz-Birkenau, the infamous extermination camp. It is my duty to remember them. There is no one else. I don't have children. When I pass away, the family ends. I have a niece and a nephew, and my late husband has one sister with two children. But it's not the same. I recorded my story for the Holocaust Memorial Museum in Washington, and I am giving the museum the one photograph I have. The recording and that

When I pass away, the family ends.

picture are the only record of my family. It is important to know what happened to them, so that mankind will learn what hatred can do. I don't want it to be like my parents never existed.

I am seventy-six years old, and my entire life has been defined by not having parents. I never had a transition from childhood to adulthood. From one minute to the next, I was grown up. I had to live with whatever decisions I made, however stupidly. I was on my own; I had to fend for myself.

For a while I was sad and pessimistic. I said, "It's not worth-while. Everything is gone. What good is it? What good am I?" But I had to find an inner strength and learn to cope, because I could not change what happened. I had no choice. Life goes on, and all you can do is try your best and be a better human being.

I TURNED AROUND AND THEY WERE GONE

My idyllic childhood came to an end when the Germans marched into Czechoslovakia in 1939. I had been a privileged child in an upper-middle-class Jewish family. We were very comfortable; my grandparents had a chauffeur and a villa, and my father was a pharmacist. My mother stayed home with me and my sister, Eva, who was three years older. I was the tomboy of the family.

My father had been a high-ranking officer in World War I for the Austro-Hungarian army, and he never believed the stories we heard. We were given the chance to flee to Switzerland, but we didn't go. He did not think the war would affect us.

The day the police came for us, in May of 1944, my parents, grandmother, aunt, my sister, and I were together in our apart-ment. At first, we didn't know what was happening, so we weren't scared. We were simply stunned. We had no time to think. We marched on foot to a holding place. We had only the clothes we were wearing. The police examined us to make sure we weren't hid-ing any jewelry or anything. Then they took us to what used to be a brick factory and was now called a ghetto. There were already many people there; family after family was in the open space of that factory. I recall that my grandmother was hungry, but there was no food. We found out that we were waiting for a train to come and ship us directly to Auschwitz.

The trains arrived, and we were starting to board when the police came and took my sister and me to a neighboring barracks, the quarters for the police. I was fourteen and my sister was seventeen. We were frightened to death. They made us undress. They never touched us, but they made us stand there, naked, for hours, while they laughed and made dirty jokes. Finally, they made us put our clothes back on and leave.

We were put immediately into a cattle car with our family. It was crowded and noisy. After days of travel, we arrived in Auschwitz. Josef Mengele was waiting for us with German shepherds. Right then and there he made the selection. First he chose my father, then my grandmother. They were sent to the left, to what I now know were the gas chambers. We never had a chance to embrace them or say goodbye. I turned around and they were gone.

I never saw my father or grandmother again. For a long time my sister and I told ourselves that they were alive in a separate part of the camp. Later, when it sank in that my father was gone, it was dreadful. I tried to imagine his face and what had happened to him. But it was so painful.

Mengele asked my mother and my aunt, who were in their late thirties, "Can you walk? Can you run?" They both said "yes," so they went with my sister and me to the right. We were all in a daze. Everything was so fast; it was noisy, the dogs were barking. We were taken to what they called the showers, where they shaved our heads, took away our clothes, gave us somebody else's horrible rags to wear, and shipped us to the barracks. This took the whole night.

I am seventy-six years old, and my entire life has been defined by not having parents.

We arrived at the barracks the following morning. We lived in those barracks from May until October. All of us slept together in the same bunk like sardines. At five o'clock every morning we were herded outside and counted. We stood there for hours. Every day there were selections to decide who would live and who would die. For no good reason, people were sent to one side or the other.

Mengele knew well that families stuck together, so he purposely divided them when he found out. One day in October we made a fatal mistake. He figured out that we were related, and he sent my mother and sister to the left, my aunt and me to the right.

The next thing I knew, my mother and sister were gone, and my aunt and I were being marched away. Again, there was no chance to say goodbye.

The last time I saw my mother was no different than any other morning we were sent out. We were standing together one moment, and the next moment she was gone.

I didn't realize the enormity of it. I just thought we were being separated for some reason. The following day was my sister's birthday. We were saving a little ration of bread for her birthday. We never got to give it to her.

The entire time I was in Auschwitz, I thought my parents were alive. I never thought they weren't. Even after the war, I dreamed that eventually my parents would come. In my mind we would all be reunited, my mother and father and sister. I just didn't know when and where.

TIME DOES NOT HEAL

After my aunt and I were separated from my mother and sister, we were once again put on a train. We didn't know whether we were heading for the gas chambers or somewhere else. After traveling the whole night, we arrived at a work camp in Poland. Our job was to dig ditches. It was cold; they herded us out early in the morning wearing almost nothing and gave us shovels that were heavier than I was. We were emaciated, skin and bones. We had to stand there the whole day and try to dig, and then at night they herded us back into the cold, miserable barracks and gave us some small amount of food.

My aunt was with me the whole time. And she was wonderful. As a friend of mine says, God looked down and saw that I didn't have my mother, so he gave me an aunt. When I was freezing, she took my hands into her mouth to warm them.

We stayed in that work camp until the Russians were close; we could hear the guns. Then we were forced to evacuate. I know it was after Christmas because at Christmastime we saw that the soldiers' barracks were decorated, and the beautiful smells of food tortured us. We were taken on a death march through one village after another. Those who couldn't march were shot by the side of the road. At night we slept in barns with horses and cattle, and in the morning they herded us back onto the road. Finally, one night my aunt couldn't go any further. She told me, "Go ahead, and leave me behind. I know they will shoot me, but I have to take my chances." She kissed me goodbye and then hid under the straw, and I left her there.

In the morning, dogs were sent out to find people who were hiding. Many were found and punished. But miraculously, I later learned, the dogs didn't sniff her out. After the guards left, she went to a nearby village and, in her perfect German, told people that she was the widow of a soldier and was bombed out of Dresden. She survived the rest of the war with a family there.

Now I was alone on the death march. How on earth was I able to survive it? I don't know. The survival instinct is strong, but the brain suffers when you are malnourished. You don't think clearly. I wasn't thinking of my mother and father then; I was simply trying to march. I didn't think of them until much later. We marched for weeks until we got to Bergen-Belsen, another camp. That was where, on April 15, 1945, I was liberated. I had been in the camps for almost a year.

To this day I bear many scars from my experience. I detest trains; I have an immediate flashback to the train to Auschwitz. I can't stand German shepherds. When my husband and I were looking for apartments in New York, he found one and asked me to come and see it. It was on Park Avenue, facing the East River. It was terrific until I opened the window and saw the chimneys of Con Edison, the local power company. I couldn't live there; immediately it brought back the memories of the chimneys at the death camp.

The Holocaust had such a tremendous impact on my psyche that it will never go away. Everything I am comes from living without my parents for so long. Time does not heal. My pain is still strong, and it stings still. I live with it day in and day out; it will forever be a part of me.

OUT OF THE ASHES

After the war, I went back to Czechoslovakia and found my aunt. I was a wreck. I was fifteen, but I looked like I was seven. I was physically immature for my age. I had been in and out of hospitals; I had symptoms of menopause, including hot flashes, and didn't get my period for three more years. Later, as an adult, I could not get pregnant. It didn't matter to me, though; I didn't want to bring a child into a world where this kind of horror might happen again.

To this day, I can still hear my parents' voices in my head.

Ultimately, I made my way to America and met my husband. It was dreadful not to have my parents at my wedding. I had a small wedding because I felt the absence of my family so strongly. At my wedding, my mother-in-law called my husband Fred aside and said, "You must be extra nice to Catheryne because she has no parents to run home to." It was a beautiful thing to say to him.

It has always been painful at holidays, and now it is doubly so because my husband is also gone. I am blessed with wonderful friends who assure me that I am part of their extended family. They insist that I celebrate with them, which is lovely. My greatest joy is to see the future generation, especially the children of my friends who are survivors. To see their children growing up gives me immense pleasure. Out of the ashes, there is new life.

I NEVER STOPPED BELIEVING IN GOD

It is useful to talk to people who have been through similar experiences, and for that reason I belong to a group of survivors. Losing your parents under such traumatic conditions shapes your whole being and your whole outlook on life.

I think it is also important to do some good, to get involved. Many of us who survived the Holocaust are either in health service or social work. I volunteer at Memorial Sloan-Kettering Cancer Center. I am a breast cancer survivor myself, and I work in the chemotherapy section, talking to patients while they're getting chemo, answering questions, and encouraging them. I have forged close ties with many patients beyond the clinic. I was recently awarded the Volunteer of the Year medal. It gives me great satisfaction to know that I can help others.

My parents are still an integral part of my life. There isn't a day that I don't think of them in one way or another. Just recently I was in a cosmetic store and saw a brand of face powder that my mother used. The minute I saw it, I had a vision of my mother sitting at her dressing table using it. A million and one things are a constant reminder. To this day I can still hear my parents' voices in my head.

I don't come from a religious background. We were quite assimilated in Czechoslovakia, and I don't even have a Hebrew name. Since I don't know when my parents perished, I say Kaddish (the Jewish prayer of mourning) for them on their birthdays. I say prayers, but not in a religious sense. I pray that God will be with my family in heaven and give them eternal peace.

I never stopped believing in God.

Jeff Gelman

JEFF GELMAN
I Had to Find My Own Way and Grow Up Fast

MY ENTIRE LIFE is defined by what happened to me when I was fourteen. In a single moment, everything changed. My parents were killed by a drunk driver. I had been raised in a caring, loving environment where I always felt safe and comfortable. After my parents died, I was thrown into an entirely new world. I couldn't count on anyone or anything.

The people my parents had named in their will as my guardians, their close friends Harriet and Robert Finkelstein, were in the car with them. Robert was also killed. After the crash I went to live with Harriet, but it didn't work out. By the time I graduated from high school, I had lived in three households and gone to four different high schools. I had to find my own way and grow up fast.

I am now thirty-two years old, and for a long time I haven't gotten any great enjoyment from my birthdays or holidays. When my parents were alive, those had been joyous times, and after they died, celebrating them became difficult. Now that I have two small children of my own, I hope my feelings will begin to change.

I have now been alive longer than I was ever my parents' son. For many years I couldn't think about my parents without being sad. I couldn't talk about them. I shut down, hid in my room, and didn't want to talk to anybody. Once you have that kind of major loss, you mentally prepare yourself so you don't get hurt again. You don't want to feel vulnerable, so you try not to open yourself up to intimate relationships. I still have a hard time getting close to people.

IT DIDN'T SEEM REAL

Sometime after ten o'clock on a Saturday evening—late enough that it was kind of strange—the phone rang. I had been visiting my friend Dave for a week, and my parents were staying overnight with their friends, the Finkelsteins, on their way to pick me up. I didn't know it at the time, but my friend Dave went downstairs to find out who called and learned that my parents had been killed, and then had to come back upstairs and pretend nothing was wrong. His parents didn't want to tell me yet. Their reasoning was, "There's no point in telling him now. Give him one last night of sleep. We'll tell him in the morning."

I couldn't count on anyone or anything.

I thought that was a good thing for a long time. But now I'm not so sure. Dave's father woke me up early the next morning and led me downstairs. I was confused. I knew my parents weren't there yet. I didn't understand why he was waking me up, and why Dave was still in bed. Dave's mom was on the living room couch, crying.

She said that there was a terrible accident the night before, and my parents and their friend had been killed on their way out to dinner.

I felt a slow building of fear and then uncontrollable shivering. Dave's mom told me that it was okay to cry, so I did—because she suggested it and because I was scared. They wrapped me in a blanket and bundled me in the car. I couldn't stop shivering, no matter how high they turned the heat up. It didn't seem real. I thought, "Maybe my parents will be there when I arrive."

When we got to the Finkelsteins' house, it was total chaos. There were dozens of people; the phone was ringing, people were crying. A few hours later Dave's parents took me to the hospital, where a nurse handed me a manila envelope containing my mom's purse. Quickly, I went through the contents: My parents' wallets, sunglasses, reading glasses, change, pens, my dad's cigarettes and lighter, even my parents' wedding bands. I had braced myself, thinking that they might have blood all over them, but they were clean. Rifling through their possessions felt like a violation of their privacy, especially with everyone watching.

The nurse asked if I wanted to see my parents' bodies. I said yes. I needed to get real in my head that this had happened. *My parents are really dead.* I needed to see the evidence. I started to go with her, but Dave's dad put his hand on my shoulder and said, "I don't think that's a good idea. They're not going to be how you remember them," so I didn't go.

Now I have mixed feelings about not seeing my parents. It might have been good for me to understand that they were really dead, as opposed to holding out hope that they were still alive somewhere, and that this had been a mistake. But having the image in my head of them severely injured would have been traumatic.

I JUST SHUT DOWN

My house was also filled with friends and relatives. Everyone was staring at me. They didn't know what to do with me, whether to say something or not. My aunt eventually led me upstairs to my room and talked about how important it was to let out my emotions—throw things, scream, punch the walls, stomp around. But I couldn't. I didn't want people to worry or feel pity for me. I didn't want to draw attention to myself.

At my parents' funeral, people I'd never met before were coming up and hugging me, saying they were sorry. It made me really uncomfortable; I wished they had just left me alone. Afterward my aunt told me, "In their will, your parents said they wanted you to live with Robert and Harriet Finkelstein. But with Robert gone we're not sure what's going to happen. Even if you still want to live with Harriet, her family is shattered right now, and we don't know if she can take you."

For the next few weeks, my aunt, uncle, and grandmother lived with me in my house. I pretty much stayed in my room. I had a cat, so he kept me company. I read a lot of comic books and just kind of shut down. I slept late and then took long naps. Eventually I went back to school, to try to create a semblance of a normal life for myself. Kids who used to tease me came up and said they were sorry. Others looked at me in the halls, and I wondered what they were thinking. I didn't want anyone feeling sorry for me. And I felt uncomfortable in class. I couldn't do my homework, couldn't concentrate, couldn't focus. So I stopped going.

My parents' belongings were slowly disappearing. The house was getting barer and barer; pictures and art objects and books and furniture were being given away. I didn't like it, but I was so overwhelmed I didn't know what to do. There were only two things I really wanted. One was my dad's tape recorder. The Finkelstein boys and I used to pretend that we were putting on a newscast; one of us did the news, one sports, and one the weather. My dad would let me use his tape recorder for that. So I thought I'd be able to have it when I moved in with them. But my uncle wouldn't let me; he thought I would break it. I also wanted one of my parents' cars. I hoped to drive it in two years when I had my license. My uncle nixed that idea too. He thought it was impractical.

My parents' belongings were slowly disappearing.

I SERIOUSLY CONSIDERED SUICIDE

When I finally moved in full-time with the Finkelsteins, I was relieved. But grief had changed things in their household. The kids had just lost their father, too. I had already switched schools and had been going there for a few months when Harriet sat me down and said, "This isn't working out." She suggested boarding school—one of the options I had considered before I moved in.

Everyone, including me, had said "no way." But when things get desperate, you take desperate measures.

I had high hopes for boarding school. I imagined it would be a place where other outcasts were, kids who didn't have families. I thought it might be a bonding experience. But it wasn't like that at all. Some kids took full advantage of the fact that I was fairly defenseless. I was alone, withdrawn, and depressed. I felt like everyone had abandoned me. Harriet thought it would be best for me to come home every month or so. My uncle was giving me a hard time because my grades weren't perfect; I was getting B's and C's. I seriously considered suicide. But I thought it would be wimpy to cop out. That's not what my parents would have wanted. I didn't want to let them down.

All through boarding school I secretly wished that my parents would come and get me. It was so difficult to fathom that they were gone. At the time they died, they had already been out of my life for a week, so their absence just seemed like an extension of that. I thought they'd come back at some point, and I'd just hold things together until then. When I was at my lowest point, I realized that if they were going to come get me, they would've gotten me by now. They wouldn't have let me go through this. I had to accept that they weren't coming.

My aunt knew how miserable I was and arranged for me to move in with a distant cousin and his family in Pennsylvania. It was only my sophomore year, and I was about to go to my fourth high school. But it turned out to be a small, nurturing environment. The family provided me with a great deal of stability and helped me turn my life around.

LET GO OF BLAME

One of the things I have learned in this experience is to never give up hope, because things are going to get better eventually. You just have to get through it. At boarding school I spent a lot of time in my memories. When I moved to Pennsylvania I still wasn't talking about my parents to anyone, but at least I was beginning to deal with the fact that they were gone.

Another thing I learned is to let go of blame. The drunk driver who killed my parents spent ten years in jail and then was released. He had been convicted of driving drunk two previous times. I almost never think about him. I didn't want to know who he was. I didn't hate him; I just didn't care about him. And that helped me. You think that you'll be satisfied by having the person rot in jail; you wish them pain or death, but even if you get your wish, you'll never get the satisfaction you want.

I have now been alive longer than I was ever my parents' son.

A cousin of my mother's told me, "If you don't talk about this, someday you're going to be in trouble." I was sent to one therapist after another, but I just couldn't talk about it until I was ready. I was afraid it would be too much to handle. But I wish I had gone to a grief support group. Just hearing other people talk and knowing that I was not alone, that other people were going through tough times, too, would have been a tremendous help to me.

THE TURNING POINT

I made a conscious decision that college was not going to be like boarding school; no matter what happened I was going to have a good experience. I found someone I loved who was able to provide me with a great deal of support—Lisa, the woman I married. She was the first person I felt free to talk about things with. Finally I was breaking out of my depression and gaining confidence in who I was and what I could do. It was the turning point for me.

Lisa's father passed away from cancer when she was in high school. So at our wedding, we had a moment of silence for our loved ones who could not be with us. That was how we honored them.

I have my parents' wedding rings still. I wore them on a chain around my neck when I got married, underneath my tuxedo. I keep them in a drawer in my desk. I also have my mom's purse. All in all I have two full cardboard boxes of my parents' stuff. And every once in a while, as I move from house to house or am alone at night, I pull out the boxes and go through them and just touch them. It makes me feel closer to my parents.

There are very few times when I feel sad anymore.

Kate Carlson Furer

KATE CARLSON FURER
The Wedding

MY HUSBAND, LARRY, DECIDED to ask me to marry him on the beach in Fire Island, New York on July 26, 1997. Three months earlier, my mother had been diagnosed with stage-four cancer; it was in her liver and lungs. Larry wanted to include my parents in the engagement, in case my mother couldn't make it to the wedding.

So without my knowledge, he called my mother and asked her for permission to marry me. She said yes. Then he arranged to have my older brother, David, bring my parents out to Fire Island to secretly watch him propose. As soon as they arrived, Larry got down on his knees and brought out the ring. My parents and Larry's parents watched it all unfold from the walkway leading to the beach. Then he said, "I really love you," and pointed up, and there they were.

It was absolutely amazing to have my mother be a part of that.

She was having chemotherapy at the time, and everything went relatively well for a while. We were going to get married in May of the following year; we thought she would make it that long. But by the fall I was leaving my Manhattan apartment to go out to New Jersey three times a week and every weekend to take care of her. I did all the shopping, the cooking, and the cleaning because my dad couldn't; he'd been suffering from Parkinson's disease for years.

By Thanksgiving weekend, we knew that my mom wasn't going to make it to the wedding. So I decided to pick out everyone's gown quickly: the bridesmaids', my flower girl's, and my mother's—and then we started making phone calls and moved the wedding up six months—from mid-May to December 21. My mother went with me to pick out my wedding gown, and I bought the first one I tried on.

By the time the wedding day arrived, my mother had been home, in hospice care, for a few weeks. But on my wedding day, she was the strongest she had been in a long time. Even though she was confined to a wheelchair, she looked beautiful and was so happy. She was full of smiles. My mother had always loved family gatherings. She was the glue of the family and everyone came to see her. It was nice—her last big party. I have a picture of her in that wheelchair, being escorted down the aisle by my three brothers, and right behind her there seems to be a halo, a beautiful light that stretches from one shoulder to the other.

Some people plan their weddings for years. I did mine in three weeks.

I think that God was looking over everything, because it went so smoothly. Some people plan their weddings for years in advance, and I did mine in three weeks. We had 170 people from all over—Washington State, Florida, the coast of Maine. Everyone somehow got there because they knew it was the last time they would see her.

I'm happy that I was able to give my mother this wonderful send-off. She knew I was going to be married and okay.

She died two months later.

I WASN'T PREPARED

The day before she died, she slept a lot more than usual. I was there, watching over her. The next morning I went back into Manhattan as usual. I had to get some things done for work. In the early afternoon, I received a call from my brother John. He said, "We're coming down to the end," so I turned around and went right back.

My mother was breathing, but you could see that it was much harder for her. You could talk to her, but she was not able to talk back. My father, my brother John, and Larry and I were all there when she died. I was holding her hand and talking to her, telling her how wonderful she was.

I was distraught when my mother died. She was sixty-eight years old, and I had just turned twenty-nine. Even though I knew she was going to die, when it happens you still are not prepared. I remember my brother John bending down and holding her hand, and I kissed her. I was very upset; I screamed and cried.

My brothers had already made the funeral arrangements. My mother was buried in the gown she wore to my wedding.

OUT OF NOWHERE

In the year after my mother died, my relationship with my dad got stronger. It had to. I'd always had a close bond with my mother; if there was a day we didn't see each other, we'd speak on the phone. So I built a relationship with my father that I hadn't really had before. I went out to his house every other weekend and spoke to him more than ever.

During that year, every single day I would cry. Then, the Friday before the one-year anniversary of my mother's death, I decided I was set for recovery. It was time. I went to the bookstore and purchased a book about mothers and daughters. Then, out of nowhere, my father died.

I was at work, and I just knew something was wrong. I had that feeling. I went downstairs to get an iced tea and then came back upstairs to the receptionist, who told me my brother John had just called. I called him at work and at home, and he didn't answer. Then I called him at our parents' home. When John picked up the phone I said, "Don't even tell me," and he said, "Yes."

My father wanted to die. He was seventy-eight, and I believe he died of a broken heart, not Parkinson's.

We had to go back to the same funeral home and pick everything out again. It felt like the worst case of déjà vu. We had to make the same phone calls to the same people we had called a year before about my mom. I couldn't believe what I was doing. This time I was a little more involved; my brothers had taken control over my mother's funeral as a way of protecting me. But now I picked out the casket. It was important to me to have a say.

My father died a year after my mother—just one week apart. Both passed away on a Monday and were buried on a Saturday.

THAT ORPHAN FEELING

Right after my father died, in the beginning, I felt like, *Why did this happen to me? What did I do to deserve this?* Most of my friends have both parents, and some even have their grandparents. I was thirty years old at the time, and both my parents were gone.

I was much younger than my brothers were, and I felt that I had gotten thrown out of the bird's nest. I wish my husband and I could have bought our first house before they died, and invited my parents over for Thanksgiving or a holiday. I missed out on that.

The hardest thing about both of my parents being gone is that I can't ask anyone, "What did I do when I was two years old?" Was I nervous to start preschool?" The link to my childhood is gone.

My brother Billy had his first son when I was ten, and the next when I was eleven, and the next when I was twelve. He had all these kids, and my parents were involved in all their birthdays and any big events. I definitely feel some resentment because my parents were so involved with my brothers' children; they baby-sat and were always there. And I got none of that.

My husband's parents and all his grandparents were still living when I buried both of my parents. Sometimes I felt angry—it wasn't fair. There I was having dinner with them, and I was really suffering, and everyone else was having a good time. I still feel resentful. And my husband is Jewish, and I'm not, so I felt like I couldn't even celebrate my own religious holidays. It's hard to keep your own religion going when that connection—your parents—is gone.

You go day by day; I saw a therapist. And my husband supported me a lot. But it wasn't easy.

When I gave birth to my daughter, Catherine, it was lonely because I didn't have any of my family around; it was all my husband's family. It was upsetting. That's when you feel that orphan feeling, and you wish you had your family back.

IT'S BEEN SIX YEARS SINCE WE'VE SPOKEN

After my father passed away, my three brothers and I sat down at the table to talk about how to divide our parents' things. My brother John felt that he was entitled to my father's company because he had worked there. So we gave it to him.

When you have several children, though, there's always going to be one child who's a bit needier. Everything was going to be divided up equally, but John felt he should receive more—meaning the business, the property, and buying *I lost my brother* out the other partner. In addition to that, *over money.* he *then* wanted to split the remaining assets equally among all four of us. We were willing to give him the business, but we felt that if he wanted to buy out the partner, he should use part of his inheritance. Billy, my other brother, tried to speak to him about different approaches, different ideas, but John wanted only his way. So he got up and left. It became a very hard battle.

Not only did I lose my parents, but I lost John. It's been six years since we've spoken.

John was actually the brother I was closest to. He took me and my other siblings to court a year ago, and he wouldn't really even speak to us there either. He yelled at me and told me how selfish he thought I was. I always thought my brother John was the type of person you could rely on; he was good and caring and loving. And then, all of a sudden, he just turned.

All of us have called him, trying to talk to him. But the only way he would speak to us was if we went to his side. I never even got an acknowledgment that I was having a baby. My daughter was born on the same day as his daughter, and he never even called or sent a note.

One thing I've learned from all of this is that you have to speak about wills and make sure that your children know where you stand. Don't leave anything up in the air. I lost my brother over money.

THE RESPONSIBILITY OF CHRISTMAS

Every single holiday, I put flowers next to my parents' headstones—even for Valentine's Day and Halloween. And when it's Christmas, I bring a laminated card, to withstand the weather. I bring Catherine, who is now four, to the gravesite and take pictures of her there. I have a picture on my dresser of her putting flowers on my parents' graves from the last time we went.

I try to keep Christmas traditions alive. My mother and I always made chocolate chip cookies for Christmas; hers were amazing, and I make them the same way. My daughter knows that those are from my mother. I also have ornaments from my mother. When I put them up, I tell Catherine that these are from my mommy's tree and they're very precious. And I always give Catherine a special gift for Christmas and say it's from my parents. Because my husband is Jewish, the responsibility of making sure Catherine gets a sense of the Christmas tradition falls to me. I carry that alone.

Catherine calls my parents Grandma and Pampa. She talks about them, which is nice. As she gets older, I will definitely talk about my parents more.

I think it's important to have pictures around so that when your children grow up, you can tell them who their grandparents were and what they did. When my mother passed away, I made a collage of pictures of her, and Catherine has that in her room. And jewelry—I wear my mother's wedding band every day. On holidays, birthdays, and anniversaries, I wear her engagement ring. I even kept some of her clothes.

TIME DOES HEAL

In the beginning, after my parents died, I thought about them every single day. When my father passed away, somebody told me, "Time will heal you," and even though I didn't want to hear it at the time, it's true—time does heal.

I don't think about my parents every single day anymore. It's more on special occasions, like their anniversary and birthdays. I choose to light a candle and say a prayer for them, and there are times when I still cry, but I don't fall apart.

Terrance Dean

TERRANCE DEAN
Grieving for What I Never Had

THE LAST TIME I SAW my mother, she was dying of AIDS. I was in college, and I stayed with her for two weeks during my Christmas break. She was wasting away, getting smaller, and she was in pain. I would help her get out of bed and eat. I made sure that she had everything she needed and was comfortable.

People who are in the final stages of AIDS look like they've lost part of themselves. It's like they're preparing for death. Mentally and physically, they begin to change. They become calmer and more reflective. During that time, we were able to talk. As I was leaving her apartment, my mother told me she loved me. She'd never said it before. I'm sure she knew it was the last chance she would ever have to say it. I told her I loved her, too. I knew she was thinking, *I'm complete now. I told my son I love him, and he loves me.*

She died a month later, in February. My grandmother called me at college and told me. I hung up the phone and cried. I took it really hard when I went home and saw her in the casket. I was twenty-one, and even though my father had died years earlier, it was my first time seeing someone dead. It suddenly hit me: She isn't here anymore. I'll never speak to her again.

When I was younger, I used to tell my mother, "I wish you were dead." So I felt responsible, like I caused my mother's death. All kids say they hate their parents at some point, but I wish I'd never said it.

ANGER

My mother was a prostitute and a drug addict. For a long time, I despised her. I wouldn't speak to her. I lived with my grandmother, my mother's mother, and when my mom would come to visit, I would shy away.

At the time, I was about eight years old, and I didn't understand what was going on. I just knew that Mommy wasn't there. But a moment came when I was fourteen and I understood. I was with kids from the neighborhood, playing in the water from a fire hydrant. It was summer. My mother came outside with a T-shirt on and

When I grieve for my parents, I'm also grieving for what I never had.

some really short shorts and got in the water with us. Her T-shirt got wet, and she wasn't wearing a bra. A group of men on a porch were saying things like, "We can pay for that." Suddenly I understood how men looked at my mother. I understood what my mother was. I wanted her to go in the house. I was extremely embarrassed and angry. Why couldn't she be like the other moms in the neighborhood?

Despite all the anger I felt toward my mother, I also felt a burden to please her, to make her happy. I wanted to be good for Mommy. I thought, *Look at all these great things I'm doing as your child—will that make you stop using drugs? Will you stop being a prostitute if I'm a good boy?* Deep down I thought maybe it was my fault; maybe she was doing all that because she didn't want to have children.

After my mom died, I wanted to run as far away as possible. I wanted to escape from the whole family. As angry as I was at her, I was just as angry with the rest of my family. I thought, *At what point did you guys step in? Why didn't you try to do some kind of intervention and get help?* My anger was spread out equally among everyone.

Years later, my grandmother told me that her son, my mother's brother, had been killed by the Detroit police when my mother was young. Apparently my mother and he were very close, and when he died she missed him terribly. His name was Alex. My grandmother felt that my mother resorted to drugs, and then the street, after Alex died. Talking with my grandmother gave me a better understanding of what might have been a cause of my mother's lifestyle. I began to feel sorry for her.

My relationship with my mother is better now than it was when she was alive. I know she did the best she could. She was only trying to survive. She was addicted to drugs; selling her body was what she knew. As a child I felt, "You're supposed to be a mother to your children, but you'd rather to go in the bathroom and shoot up heroin. You wear skirts that are too short and shirts that are too low, with lots of makeup, getting dropped off by different men every day in different cars." So, in the end, our reconciliation was very healing for me.

I FEEL JEALOUS

I was twelve years old when my father died. We never had a real relationship. I knew he was my dad, but I didn't know what the word "dad" meant. I saw my friends who had dads, and I thought, *Well, that's what a dad does. He's around the home and responsible for his children. He acts like he cares.* But my father was so detached from me that I didn't see him in that capacity. He was just this man who would come to my house.

The way I found out he had died was that I was riding in a car with my grandmother to the post office when she said, "Oh, by the way—your dad was killed." Her tone bothered me; it was very blasé and casual. She told me that my father had been in a store, as a customer, and he got shot in a robbery. That's all that was said about it.

I don't know if I actually believe that story. When I talk to my relatives now, as an adult, they are still evasive about my father. I know that his name was Michael, but I don't know where he lived, where he came from, or anyone in his family. I didn't go to his funeral, and I don't know where he is buried. My mother's family won't give me the details. It's a void. Everyone tells me I have the same mannerisms as my father; we're the same height and look similar. But I don't have any photographs of him.

I don't miss my father. I feel more resentful toward him, like, "How dare you not be a part of my life? How dare you not step up to the plate?" I have all these questions. When I was sixteen, a man who owned a convenience store in my neighborhood became a father figure to me. It was the first time an adult male had shown any

I feel resentful toward him, like, "How dare you not be a part of my life?"

interest in me. I worked for him, and I was in his store every day. He paid attention to me. He cared. He would invite me into his home to hang out with him and his son, who was my age. I'd watch them interacting with each other. The father would talk, and then listen; it was like a dance they had. And even though I felt close to his son, like he was a cousin, I felt envious. I'd think, *I wish that were me.*

When I grieve for my parents, I'm also grieving for what I never had. When I hear about other people's relationships with their parents, I feel jealous. A good friend of mine still has his parents, and he's close to both of them. He talks about his family all the time. I can hear myself in my head, the envy I have of him. I don't want to hear him talk about his parents.

I don't call myself an orphan. My grandmother and other people stepped in, and my parents' presence wasn't all that strong to begin with. But I do wish I'd known what a relationship would have been like with a mother and a father.

ABANDONED BY TWO PARENTS

I am extremely lonely. I didn't have a close relationship with my parents, so I didn't learn how to express my emotions. I learned to close off that side of me; I became emotionless. As an adult, it's still hard for me to relate to people intimately. My friends tell me that I have a hard shell around me. I spend a lot of time alone. It's about abandonment. Even though my mom was alive, I felt abandoned by two parents. People are going to leave anyway, so why get attached? Why get close? I loved my mom, and I felt kicked around by her and what she was doing. I can be in the company of people, but I can't be with them intimately. I feel like running away all the time.

MY LOVE CAME VERY LATE, BUT AT LEAST IT CAME

What helped me in dealing with losing my mother was being able to tell her that I loved her at the eleventh hour. I've heard many people say they wish they could have said that. I had the opportunity to spend time with her at the end, and I took advantage of it. Every time I'm around someone with at least one living parent, I say, "What's your relationship like with your parents? Get it right. Regardless of what you may think or feel, tell them how much you love them. You never know when they won't be here any longer. Clean up unfinished business." My love came very late, but at least it came.

I still didn't want any of my mother's clothes or jewelry. Everything was still tainted for me. But fifteen years later, when my grandmother died, something unexpected happened. My cousin was cleaning out our grandmother's house and found a Bible that had letters and notes tucked into it. My mother had written them to my grandmother when she was sick. She told my grandmother how sorry she was and how she wished she had been a better daughter. The notes in the Bible asked God for forgiveness. My mother also asked God to watch over her children and to make sure we were happy.

The letters and notes mean everything to me because I always thought my mother didn't love me.

When my mother was alive, I couldn't have cared less if she was around. But now that she's not here, I wish she were. I am still overwhelmed by the enormity of not having both my parents. I keep asking myself the question, *Why me?* I wish I had known my father. I wish we'd had a relationship. It didn't have to be a great one, I just wanted to know he was here. I wish my parents could see what I've done, how I have succeeded.

My life had always been about pleasing other people. I tried to make my mother happy, and once she died, I poured all that effort into pleasing my grandmother. Their both being gone now grants me a kind of freedom. I don't have the burden to please them, to make them happy. The freedom has given me the mental space to become successful.

I had to make something happen or I would have self-destructed.

Rosanna Arquette

ROSANNA ARQUETTE
My Mom Is the Wind, and My Dad Is the Rain

MY MOM DIED when I was thirty-eight, and my dad died when I was forty-one. When they were lowering my mother's casket, I threw some sunflowers on top of it, and they were blown off by a gust of wind. So now when the wind blows, everybody in my family thinks of her. Mom is the wind.

When my dad died, it rained for three days. He is the rain.

DEATH IS A BEAUTIFUL THING

I feel my mother around a lot. One time after she died, I was feeling bad about my career, really down as an actress, depressed. I opened a drawer and found a letter from her, telling me what a great actress I was. I didn't even remember having it. She had written it a decade earlier, after she saw a production I was in. She wrote, "This is a fan letter." It was as if she had just sent it. The letter needed to be there, and I needed to get it.

When I was growing up, my mom and I had an intense relationship. She could be pretty abusive. And then she got healthy and became a therapist for women. We healed our stuff. What helps now is the knowledge that in the end, I was cleaned up and clear with both of my parents. If you have unfinished business, it's hard.

By the time they detected my mom's cancer in her breast, it had already gone into the lung. She did a couple of rounds of chemo, which made her feel ill. She decided to do an alternative route of healing. She had a very good eight years. That's a long time to live when you have terminal cancer. She found every alternative treatment you could possibly find.

It was important to my mom to have a conscious death. She didn't want to take painkillers. She didn't want to be disconnected from us. That was hard, because she was in a lot of pain. When my mom was very sick, we tried to get her to do pot to ease the pain. But she hated it; it made her cough.

Near the end of my mom's life, I was shooting a movie in Canada. I flew home on weekends; I wanted to be there when she died. I told the producers, "I need to be done with this movie. Change the schedule, do my scenes, and get me out of here." When I finished the movie, I got my stuff and went right to my mother's house. I'm the oldest of five kids, and the family was waiting for me to come to pull the plug on the ventilator, so that we could all be there. I walked in and completely fell apart.

They pulled the plug, and she miraculously lived for another ten days. It was in those ten days that everybody's stuff came out. I want to make a film of it someday. My sister Patricia and I had a huge, violent fight. She took a chair and threw it out the kitchen window. It was such intense drama and pain, and we were rarely a dramatic family. I also had a fight with my brother Richmond because I told him not to eat any oranges; they were the only thing that could get rid of my mother's hiccups. She had these horrible hiccups while she was in the coma. I said, "Those are Mom's oranges," and he said, "Get off my back." Patricia said, "What are you guys fighting about?" All that stuff needed to be dealt with. I think my mother was just waiting for us to work it out.

The night before my mom died, I slept on the floor of her bedroom. We lit a beautiful candle, and I played the Beatles. The next morning at about seven I was sitting in the kitchen and my mom's friend came in and said we should go to her room. My brother David and I went in there. Mom was gasping like a fish out of water.

I come from a spiritual family. There was a very okay feeling about death. It wasn't scary.

She was like a shell; you could tell she was not truly there anymore. She was above, looking at us. We said, "Mom, it's okay for you to let go. We'll be okay. We love you, Mom; let go." We just held her in our arms, and she died.

I come from a spiritual family. There was a very okay feeling about death. It wasn't scary. There were so many relatives and friends around who were loving and supportive, who had the consciousness that death is a beautiful thing, not an ugly thing.

Before she died, my mother said she was afraid that something would happen to her body. "Stay there and make sure that I go into the ground," she told us. In my mind I thought that guys would come in and dig the grave with shovels, but they don't do that anymore. They do it with bulldozers. And they don't want people to see that part of it, when they pound the dirt in. But we all stayed for that. I thought, "Okay, Mom, you're in."

I NEEDED TO BE CLOSE TO HER

Grieving is a process. I think you have to let yourself to do whatever you need to. After my mom died I didn't get out of bed for a week. I checked out. You have to allow yourself to have your feelings. Being stoic may be a way of covering up. It's okay to be depressed; it's normal.

They passed on an independent, artistic spirit that my daughter has and that her children will have. My parents gave that to me.

My mother died on August 5, and my birthday is August 10. The year after my mother died, I went to the cemetery on my birthday and spent the day lying on top of her grave, hanging out. I just needed to be close to her.

My mom loved amber and turquoise, and I wear pieces of them now. We all have some of her jewelry. She wore Birkenstocks before they were hip and fashionable. When I was younger I hated them. And then, when she died, I bronzed them. They're in my living room, like a sculpture. They look exactly like her footprint, exactly how she walked.

I miss my mom a lot right now. I want her to meet the new man in my life. I'm happy, and I think she would have loved him. This is the guy she had been waiting for, for me.

WE'RE ORPHANS

My father had been very sick in the hospital with complications from a liver transplant, and I knew he was going to die. David was making a movie in Arizona, and I called and said, "You need to get on a plane." From my mother's death I knew that it was important for all of us to be there at the moment of death. It had been such a beautiful experience for me and David with our mother that I wanted my other siblings to experience that with our dad.

The doctor insisted on doing one more operation to save my dad's life. The kids were okay with it—I call my brothers and sisters "the kids" because I'm the oldest—but I was against doing anything more. We had already said goodbye to him. It was emotional. We were sobbing. I went crazy. I grabbed the doctor and said, "We're the kind of family that wants to be there when he dies. We want to be with him."

My father ended up not making it.

We were all so overcome, we collapsed in the hallway outside his room, like puppies in a heap. We kept saying, "We're orphans, we're orphans." It felt empty and lonely and sad. It was such huge grief not to have both of my parents anymore.

Just days after my father died, my brothers and sisters went to clean out his apartment. Patricia is the one who takes care of everything. She organizes. She got the lawyers together and did everything right. I couldn't do it. I told them I'd send people to pack and move. They were angry with me. They didn't want to do it either, but they felt that we all needed to do it, and I should have been a part of it. I couldn't; I just wasn't ready.

THEY ARE WITH ME

My father's death, and also not having my mother anymore, affected my life in many ways. It pushed me into changing my career. I don't think it was a conscious decision; it just sparked a feeling to make a change. My mother had always told me I was going to be a director. She nurtured all her kids to be artists. Six days after my father died, I started working on a film that I would direct, *Searching for Debra Winger.* My mom would have loved the movie. At the end of the film, I thank my parents "for teaching me to break through to the other side." They passed on an independent, artistic spirit that my daughter has and that her children will have. My parents gave that to me.

The process of grieving takes a long time. Sometimes it truly hurts. For the first year after my mother died, my brothers and sisters had vivid dreams about her, like visitations. I never had one. "I want Mom to visit me," I said. "Mom, why are you not visiting me?" I was so bummed. But despite her never coming to me in a dream, I can feel her. She's around. And my dad is definitely around, for sure.

My mom is the wind, and my dad is the rain. They are my angels; they are with me.

Hope Edelman

HOPE EDELMAN
Just Seventeen

THE MORNING MY MOTHER went into the hospital for the last time, my father asked me if I could watch her. He'd been taking care of her at home during that last week, and he asked me if I would stay with her, because he needed to go talk with a rabbi. That was when I knew she was going to die. My father was a very secular man—born Jewish, but not the kind of man who would consult with a rabbi on just any matter, so I knew it was really serious.

I stayed home with her and took care of her myself for about two and a half hours. That was probably the only time in the whole course of her illness that I had full responsibility for her. It was utterly traumatic. It was so much more than I could handle. She couldn't walk by herself, and she kept asking me to bring her to the bathroom, and she was vomiting. I didn't know what to do, and I was terrified. It left a lasting impression on me, to be with someone that sick in a position of responsibility. I had just turned seventeen, and I was a young seventeen.

Before that, I had been helping out as needed—driving her to chemotherapy or helping out if she didn't feel well. It was kind of mechanical, because it didn't even enter my consciousness that she was dying. We all treated it with such optimism. She'd go and get a CAT scan, and the cancer would show up in her bones, in her lungs, and she would come home happy and say, "They did a CAT scan, and it's clear." I don't think she was lying to us; I think that's what she really believed. I think that's what she was told.

This time was entirely different because I knew she was going to die. She was crying and pleading with me—"Please tell me I'm not dying." And I knew she was. I didn't want to tell her because I realized then that no one had been telling her. All this information was coming so fast. It was complete overload. I went into shock. I remember numbing out and staying that way probably for the next couple of years.

When a child is not told how sick a parent is and then the parent dies, even if it's of a terminal illness, the child experiences it as a sudden death. You don't have any time to prepare at all, even if the body is declining.

My father called the ambulance to take her to the hospital when he got home from the rabbi's. While we were waiting for the ambulance, he sat down with me. That's when he told me, point-blank, "She's going to the hospital, and she's not going to come back." That's exactly how he said it. He never used the word "die." Obviously, that was implicit. Even though I knew it before, having that validation made it real. I wanted to turn the clock back so that I didn't have to believe it.

I didn't cry. I went into a superficial zone of dead emotion. I realized that something was going horribly wrong and that somebody had to hold it together.

We got to the hospital, and he went to do all the paperwork. I stayed with her in the ER, and he later told me that I would need to get my sister, who was at summer camp in Connecticut, several hours away. I called the camp and said, "My mother's very, very sick; she's in the hospital. I need to come get my sister tomorrow morning. Make sure she's ready."

One of my closest friends drove with me the next morning in my father's car. When we got there, we found out that they had let my sister go on a tubing trip on the Housatonic River. That was the moment when I lost faith in all adults. I felt like, *Here I am, I'm seventeen and dealing with this huge responsibility, and I'm surrounded by idiots.* It shaped my perception of authority figures for a long time afterward. I walked into the camp director's office and said, "I cannot believe you let her go on a tubing trip. I called and told you that my mother was in the hospital and I had to come and get her." And he said, "Oh, Hope, I'm sure your mother's going to be fine." That was the breaking point. I started screaming at him, "She's not going to be fine; she's dying,

> *I realized that something was going horribly wrong and that somebody had to hold it together.*

and my sister might not get to see her because you let her go on that tubing trip!" The camp director just went white. I had never exploded at an adult like that before. But I think all the anger, and all the pressure and responsibility, came pouring out. I'm being patronized by an adult who's trying to tell me that this isn't as serious as I know it is. All along, I've been told that it isn't as serious as it is. And look where that brought us. Now my sister might not get to say goodbye to our mother.

The next day, I went back to the camp to get my sister. My parents' best friends drove me, because they realized at that point I was not in any state to drive a car. No one would tell my sister over the phone what was happening, so when we got there, she didn't know why I was there. It was horrible. She saw me and knew immediately that something was wrong.

My father couldn't do a lot of the things that a parent needs to step up to the plate and do. Consistently, over the years, he asked his children to do things that really were his responsibility. So I had to tell my sister what was happening. I didn't know what I was doing; I was frightened and clueless. By the time we got home, my mother had gone into a coma, and my sister never got to speak to her again.

My mother stayed in a coma for about a day and a half. We were at the hospital the whole time. My younger brother was with a neighbor. My father didn't know how to handle things. He just let my sister and me stay at the hospital. We sat in the hallway and ate our meals in the cafeteria and slept on the couches in the hall.

There was a social worker there who saw clearly that my family was not handling this well, because we didn't have any emotional help in the hospital at all. She must have seen something that looked like denial in me, although in my recollection I was very clear about what was going on—I was in shock, not denial. At one point she backed me into a corner in the hallway and said, right up in my face, "Your mother is dying, Hope." Like this was going to be helpful—like I didn't know. She pressed a pamphlet in my hand about the five stages of grief. That was all the help we got, and I've got to say, that kind of help was not particularly helpful.

My mother died at around three in the morning. My father was with her when she died, and he came out and told me. My father—the master of euphemism, God bless him—came over and woke me up and said, "It's over." And he let me go in the room. I spent a few minutes with my mother and just talked to her.

I don't remember being part of planning the funeral. I wanted to say something, but I didn't think I could pull it off. I didn't have enough time to pull myself together and write something. I hadn't slept for two nights. I remember walking behind the casket holding my brother's hand, feeling very much like I needed to take care of him on that day. And I can't remember crying, not even at the funeral. I must have. But I didn't really break down until a year later, when we did the Jewish unveiling (a graveside ceremony where the tombstone is put in place and prayers are said).

I remember crying a lot at the unveiling.

MY MOTHER NEVER KNEW

My mother was diagnosed with breast cancer when I was fifteen, and there was a great deal of deception surrounding her disease. My mother was never told exactly how sick she was. My father and her oncologist agreed that she would go in for tests, and when the results came in, the doctor would call my father. They would decide what, if anything, they were going to tell her. It's hard to believe that such a thing could go on in the medical profession; it seems horribly unethical to me today. But it did.

They thought that if she knew how sick she was, she would give up. The oncologist told me years later that the day she walked into his office and he saw her records, he knew it was not a matter of trying to save her life; it was a matter of trying to keep her alive as long as they could, because she had three children. He and my father both felt that if she were told, she would go quicker. For many years I was angry about that. But as an adult, I sat down and had a heart-to-heart conversation with her best friend, who said, "I think they were right. I think you would have lost her sooner if she knew."

What came then was a great sadness and acceptance that I would never get the kind of parenting I'd been looking for from anybody, so it was time to stop trying.

As a young woman, I walked through life with this self-righteous attitude that my mother had been wronged, and I would do things differently. I would demand to see what was under the microscope. I was adamant about being in control of my health-care. I would insist on hearing the news. But now I'm at the age she was when she was diagnosed, forty-one. As a mother with children who are still very dependent on me, I can understand why she may have made the choices she did.

I thought of my mother as an unwilling participant in the drama, when, in fact, she could have asked. She could have insisted on knowing. She could have demanded to speak with the doctor herself and not get the news from my father, and she didn't. So there was a form of collusion going on there. And I have to believe that my father and the doctor felt that they were respecting her wishes, because she could have taken a stronger stance, and she chose not to.

I wouldn't make the same choice myself; I don't have the same personality. In fact, losing her at seventeen sufficiently bolstered the parts of my personality that are more assertive and resilient and make me capable of dealing with this kind of news in a different way.

EXACTLY THE OPPOSITE

My father died a year ago, at the age of seventy-four. Something had been wrong for a while, and my brother had pushed him to go to a doctor because he noticed our father was jaundiced. Eventually he was diagnosed with an inoperable tumor and, one afternoon, I got a phone call from my father. He just said, "I've got bad news. I've got a tumor in my liver." It was a matter-of-fact conversation.

I asked for his doctor's name and phone number, and I called the doctor and had a long conversation with him. I have an uncle who's a gastroenterologist, and I called him. By the end of the day, I felt I had a lot of information.

It was pretty quick, from June until January. This kind of tumor is very lethal; it blocks your bile ducts. But he was not in good health to begin with—he didn't have the physical resources to survive longer.

Ultimately, my father's illness and death played out exactly the opposite of how my mother's had. We had all the information; my father was knowledgeable about what was happening to him. The doctor would stand at the foot of the bed and deliver the information directly to him. My father was in full control of all his medical decisions. In the end, he was the one who decided not to pursue chemotherapy because of how sick it would make him and how little chance there was of it doing any good.

My sister and I tag-teamed back and forth to New York to relieve my brother, who took on most of the responsibility for my father's care because he was the one nearby. I wish I had been closer, to help my brother. At the time, my kids were young: I had a six-year-old and a two-year-old. I couldn't leave them for long. It was difficult to keep putting them on a plane to go back and forth from Los Angeles as frequently as I needed to.

In the end, I flew with my daughters on Christmas Day, knowing it would be the last time they would see him. My husband couldn't come because his father was also sick. The hospice nurse said, "It's a really good thing you're here, because we don't expect him to make it more than seven to ten days." So we stayed for three weeks.

It was a juggling act to be there for my father and not neglect my kids, because I was the only adult they had with them. If I needed to cry, I would only do it after they went to bed at night because I didn't want to scare them or destabilize them. I was afraid that if they saw me crying, they'd get scared. So I didn't let them see my emotions during those weeks. When my husband arrived was when I really broke down.

My younger daughter, who was three at the time, still remembers when we were in New York and I was crying. It had a strong impression on her. More than even her grandfather dying was the impression of seeing me cry like that in New York.

Because my father got to die at home, with full knowledge of what was happening to him, making his own decisions, surrounded by his family, it was a very peaceful passing. I found it enormously healing. It undid a lot of the trauma from my mother's death. Her death was panicky and dramatic, and in some ways, almost violent. It was utterly disrespectful. She was in the hospital bed and didn't know what was happening to her, and no one would tell her the truth.

Because of the kind of work I do, writing about the impact of being motherless, and having the knowledge that a later loss often revives an earlier loss, I kept waiting, as my father was dying, to revisit pieces of my mother's death. But that never happened in any kind of intense or profound way. I thought, *Maybe something's wrong. Maybe I'm blocking it or don't want to go there.* But a therapist friend said, "Maybe it's possible that you have worked through your mother's death. You've been writing about it for ten years; you've been in therapy. You've put a lot of effort into understanding what happened and the impact it's had on you. Maybe there wasn't anything unprocessed left for you to deal with. Maybe you were able to go into this one and experience it fully, as a separate loss" —which I very much feel I was able to do.

I wasn't frightened of losing my father. I felt that it was the natural course of events. Certainly, I would have liked to have had him alive and happy and in our lives much longer. But I also recognize that he had made choices about his own health that he knew were going to shorten his life span, and he did them anyway. My father had not been a real parent to me for a long time. He was a symbolic parent. He was someone who gave birth to me who was of a prior generation. Our relationship was very much centered on my kids. He was more of a grandfather to my children than a parent to me. I was sad that he had to leave them—he loved them so much and got so much enjoyment from them. They were attached to him, too. So that was difficult for me. But I felt that in the past dozen years or so, my siblings and I had parented my father more than he had parented us. So I didn't feel the loss of a protector or advisor. But that's why what I *did* feel was so surprising to me. I felt the loss of the psychological protection that comes from having a parent alive—it wasn't anything real.

My father's death was a huge maturing experience for me; I felt it was time for me to grow up. As long as he was alive, in the back of my mind was the possibility that one day, he was going to become the parent I needed. After he died, the hope of getting that went with him. Then came the realization of how I'd been trying to get it from people around me, my husband or my sister or my close friends. So what came then was a great sadness and acceptance that I would never get the kind of parenting I'd been looking for from anybody, so it was time to stop trying.

MY CHILDREN DON'T HAVE GRANDPARENTS IN THEIR LIVES

When my mother died, I was dealing with my own grief and wasn't really old enough or mature enough to help my siblings through it. But when my father was dying, I was conscious that it was not only my grief I needed to be aware of, but my children's as well. And that I had to find the right balance. I couldn't focus only on them and put my own needs aside, and I couldn't get so caught up in my own needs that I ignored theirs.

A month after my father died, on what would have been his seventy-fifth birthday, we got a balloon and wrote "Happy Birthday" on it, and we went out in the yard and sang "Happy Birthday" to him and said a few things. Then we let the balloon go to heaven. It was good for my children. They did it cheerfully, and they seemed to accept that their message was going to Grandpa. We'll do it again next February.

My children live in a peculiar situation of having a mother whose main professional focus is mother loss. I'm careful about how often I introduce that into the family, except on a professional level, because they're starting to get an awareness that kids can lose mothers. I don't want them to worry about losing me. They're a little too young now to understand that I'm almost the same age my mother was when she died.

I was with my mother for seventeen years, so that gave me quite a bit to draw from in terms of parenting. I have quite a few memories of her parenting and also ideas of what I want to do the same, and what I'd like to do differently. It's challenging because I don't have her as a resource. I don't have her as a support system. My children don't have a maternal grandmother. They have a paternal grandmother, but she lives in Israel, so they rarely get to see her. In functionality, if not actuality, my children don't have grandparents in their lives. And that's a huge loss for us. I mourn the loss of that, I think, at this point more than anything.

I have a sense of relief that I don't have to go through it again. It's in my past.

My identity has been shaped so much by having to survive without my mother that elements of that inevitably find their way into my parenting. Am I who I am because my mother died, or would I have been this way had she lived? When you lose a parent young, as I did, it often accentuates elements of your personality that are already there. Typically it doesn't turn you into someone whom you would have no hope of ever becoming. Within me were probably the seeds of resilience and resourcefulness and obstinacy and assertiveness. But I was a much more timid character when she was alive.

I set high standards for myself as a mother. I have terrible anxiety about dying young and leaving them motherless, because I know firsthand how that affects a child. I also have a great desire to be the best mother I can be for them, because I know our time together could be short. I don't believe it will, but I know it's possible. So I go all out—the book reports and the birthday parties. I try to pack it all in for them so that if, God forbid, I'm not here one day, they'll have a record of all the things we did together and great memories of our time together. I am trying to supply my children with what I didn't have.

I'm a detailed record keeper so that my children will have all the information they want about their babyhood. That's one thing that I, and other women like myself, really miss having—information about what we were like as infants, information about our mother's pregnancies and labors and deliveries. My children's baby books are inches thick, full of as much information as I can find. I write essays about these subjects, and I have a book I keep of all my published work so that they'll have that record to refer to if I'm not here to give them stories.

We live in the Santa Monica Mountains, in a fire zone. Every year, when fire season starts and the Santa Ana winds start blowing, we have to pack up our fire boxes. I pack a lot of things that belonged to my mother into those boxes. Those are the things that are irreplaceable. I put her engagement album in there, her wedding ring, and the family menorah. I put in a vase, too.

The gold vase was sitting in the dining room my entire childhood. When my father moved out of the house, it was one of the things he gave me. It sits in a corner of my dining room. It's not the focal point of the room, but it's noticeable. Its shape and presence remind me very much of my mother and our childhood home.

I actually have a lot of things from my mother. I have her china; I have her jewelry box and some of her jewelry, including a thick gold wedding band with three small stones set in it. I have hardly anything from my father except for his tallis (prayer shawl). I barely ever saw him wear it—maybe at our bar mitzvahs. But I sewed it with my mother; I remember stitching part of it with her.

My siblings and I are still close to each other, but in terms of being bonded as a family since my father died, what has happened instead, from my point of view, is that they've married into families that are close, and have become very involved with their spouse's family. My father was not a strong force. He didn't host family dinners or anything like that. But when he was alive, he gave us all a reason to go to New York and be in the same place at the same time. Now there's no longer that excuse. My husband and I are close to his family, but they live far away. We don't get to see them often. So I feel that we are kind of adrift, in terms of having an extended family. It's not about emotional closeness—I speak with my siblings frequently; it's really about the holidays and the traditions.

ENORMOUSLY FREEING

It's heart-wrenching and painful and difficult to go through the loss of a parent. I have a sense of relief that I don't have to go through it again. A lot of my friends are going to have to go through this once or twice still; they have it ahead of them. And I don't; it's in my past. That's a little bit freeing—to know that I don't have that fear ahead of me.

It was also enormously freeing when I accepted that I'm not going to find anyone to parent me, and I'm not going to be able to parent myself. I'm not my own parents—but I can take care of myself. I can nurture myself. I can treat myself with the kind of respect and unconditional love that a parent could give me, whether that is to make sure I go to yoga class every Tuesday morning, or make sure that I never forget that mammogram every February, or make sure I'm the best parent that I can be. It's so individual—you have to define it on your own terms.

I think it's important to accept that the kind of parental protection and love that you lost when your parents died cannot ever come from another source. So what can you do for yourself that will approximate it in a reasonable way? How can you be good to yourself, be kind to yourself, love yourself in a way that will even come close to replicating it? I don't think we ever can. But we can come close.

AFTERWORD

MANY OF THE CONTRIBUTORS in this book spoke to me about letters they found, and in some cases rediscovered, after their parents died. These pieces of paper are true gifts—left to us by our mothers and fathers long after they are gone. The notes reach out to us with unexpected wisdom and guidance, and seem to be found in times of deep sadness and need.

After my mother died, I had the seemingly endless task of sorting through all her books, deciding which ones to keep and which ones to donate. In all honesty, I made the job endless. I was incapable of packing them into boxes without going through every single book and looking through every single page. I felt compelled to analyze each word she wrote in the margins. I wanted another chance to see her handwriting. What else could I learn about my mom in these pages? What did she choose to underline? What did she find important?

I obsessed for days. And then I found a small book of poetry with a folded piece of white paper inside. It was a poem that my

mom must have copied down in college. I could tell it was typed
on a typewriter; it had a dark jumble of letters that had corrected
a typo.

The poem below is the one I found. It obviously meant a lot to
my mom, and now means everything to me.

PAIN

Why must I be hurt?
Suffering and despair,
Cowardice and cruelty,
Envy and injustice,
All of these hurt.
Grief and terror,
Loneliness and betrayal
And the agony of loss or death—
All these things hurt.
Why? Why must life hurt?
Why must those who love generously,
Live honorably, feel deeply
All that is good—and beautiful
Be so hurt,
While selfish creatures
Go unscathed?
That is why—
Because they can feel.
Hurt is the price to pay for feeling.
Pain is not accident,
Nor punishment, nor mockery
By some savage god.
Pain is part of growth.

The more we grow
The more we feel—
The more we feel—the more we suffer,
For if we are able to feel beauty,
We must also feel the lack of it—
Those who glimpse heaven
Are bound to sight hell.
To have felt deeply is worth
Anything it cost.
To have felt Love and Honor,
Courage and Ecstasy
Is worth—any price.
And so—since hurt is the price
Of Larger living, I will not
Hate pain, nor try to escape it.
Instead I will try to meet it
Bravely, bear it proudly:
Not as a cross, or a misfortune, but an
Opportunity, a privilege, a challenge—to the God that
gropes within me.

—ELSIE ROBINSON, POET
1883–1956

SHARE YOUR STORY

MOST OF THE INTERVIEWS for this book took two to three hours to conduct. Because of the difficult subject matter, the conversations would sometimes temporarily stop midway; perhaps tears needed to be wiped away or emotions had to be brought under control.

And even though some conversations were interrupted by welcome laughter, all of them were challenging to get through. Each touched on emotions and memories that are not easily shared—especially with a stranger, as I was to nearly every one of the contributors. Many of them I now consider friends.

Maybe you would like an opportunity to tell your story, as well. There is something wonderful, if not cathartic, about giving voice to your private pain. There is also something tremendously comforting about being part of a community that truly "gets" how losing your parents affects nearly everything about you.

If you want to share your story but don't know where to begin, please feel free to use the questions in the Appendix as a guide. Then, when you are ready, post your story at: **www.alwaystoosoon.com**.

APPENDIX
Interview Questions

I USED THE QUESTIONS below to help guide my interviews. I wanted to ensure I didn't miss any basic information that was central
to each contributor's story. However, every conversation was ultimately shaped by the contributors themselves. As I listened to their
answers, as I learned more about their personal stories, I invariably
changed the direction of our discussion. Some of the most important and meaningful details in this book arose out of unexpected
detours and diversions, and could never have been anticipated.

DEATH OF THE FIRST PARENT

1. How old were you when your first parent died?
2. How old was that parent when he or she died?
3. Where were you when you found out that your parent died?
4. What was the cause of death? Was it sudden, or after prolonged illness?
5. What was your immediate reaction to the news? Sadness? Anger? Frustration? Relief?
6. How did your siblings react? Were their reactions different from yours?
7. If you are an only child, did that affect how you responded to your parent's death?

DEATH OF THE SECOND PARENT

(Note: Questions 1–7 are the same as above)

1. How old were you when your second parent died?
2. How old was your second parent when he or she died?
3. Where were you when you found out that your second parent died?
4. What was the cause of death? Was it sudden, or after prolonged illness?
5. What was your immediate reaction to the news? Sadness? Anger? Frustration? Relief?
6. How did your siblings react? Were their reactions different from yours?
7. If you are an only child, did that affect how you responded to your second parent's death?
8. Was your reaction to losing your second parent different from losing your first?
9. Was the loss of your second parent harder to deal with because he or she was your last remaining parent? Why do you think it may have been harder, if it was?

FOR CONTRIBUTORS WHO LOST THEIR PARENTS YOUNG

1. How was the death of your parent(s) explained to you?
2. Did you believe the news, or did you think it was a joke or lie?
3. If both parents were killed at the same time, who took care of you right away?
4. Who eventually became your guardian?
5. Did you have a say about where you went to live?
6. How did the rest of your family respond? Was there calm or chaos?
7. Were you able to share with others how you felt? What did your friends say? Were they helpful? Did you feel like an outcast?
8. Did you ever consider suicide?
9. What physically changed for you? Did you move? Did you have to change schools? Meet new friends?
10. Did you feel, despite the best efforts of those around you, alone?

IMPACT OF LOSING BOTH PARENTS

1. How would you describe the immediate impact your parents' deaths had on you?
2. Whatever your age now, do you feel like an orphan?
3. Do you feel that the link to your childhood is forever gone?
4. After the death of your final parent, did you feel older?
5. Do you feel alone? Do you feel alone because your parents are no longer alive? Or do you feel alone in the experience of not having both parents anymore?
6. Does anyone truly appreciate how difficult it has been for you to have lost both of your parents?
7. Do you feel lonely?
8. What challenges do you face in raising your own children without the help and guidance of your parents, their grandparents?

UNRESOLVED ISSUES

1. Did you have a good relationship with your parents?
2. If your relationship was difficult, did that make the grieving process easier or more challenging?
3. When your parents died, did you have issues between you that were left unresolved? Why didn't you address them before they died?
4. What regrets do you have about your relationship with your parents?
5. Are you angry with your parents for dying? Do you feel they left you?
6. Are you able to form lasting relationships, or do you put up barriers because of the profound losses you have experienced?

RESHAPING YOUR FUTURE

1. Have the deaths of your parents affected the course of your private and professional life?
2. What concrete changes have you made as a direct result of your parents dying?
3. How did their deaths affect the relationships you have with your own family and friends?

4. Would you be living the same life now if your parents were still living?
5. Have their deaths made you focus on your own mortality?
6. Did you learn anything about your parents after they died that affected your feelings about them?

RITUALS AND REMINDERS

1. How often do you think about your parents? Every day? On special occasions? Seldom?
2. How and when do you remember them? Are special dates marked on your calendar? Do you attend certain masses? Do you light candles? Do you say certain prayers?
3. Are there sights, sounds, or smells that spark these memories?
4. Is remembering your parents hurtful, or does it help bring them closer to you?
5. If you have children, how do you keep your parents' memories alive for them?
6. If you do not have children, how do you keep the memory of your parents alive?

OBJECTS OF AFFECTION

1. What items do you have that belonged to your parents? Why did you keep them? Do they bring you comfort?
2. Did you choose these objects for yourself, or did your parents want you to have them?
3. Did you keep these objects for yourself or for others to have?
4. Did you keep any of these items because they had a certain smell that reminded you of your parents?
5. Were you able to take pleasure from these things right after your parents died, or did it take time for you to enjoy them?
6. Have you kept all the objects you originally set aside, or have you parted with some of them?
7. Where do you have these mementos? Are they stashed away, or do you see them/use them everyday?

LESSONS LEARNED

1. What helped you the most through the grieving process?
2. Did you keep a journal? Did you talk to friends, family, or a therapist? Did you take some time for yourself?
3. Did anyone say anything to you that was particularly helpful or hurtful?
4. Did you join a support group?
5. Who gave you—or is giving you now—the best support? A spouse? A sibling? A therapist? A teacher? A friend?
6. How quickly were you able to deal with your parents' estates? Belongings?
7. What advice would you give to the readers of this book about coping with the loss of their parents?

TAKING STOCK AND MOVING ON

1. How would you assess your current state of mind about being parentless?
2. Does the pain of losing both parents sting less as you get older? Or is the pain still acute?
3. Have you come to accept their deaths?
4. What insights have you gained in going through this grief process that are important for readers to remember?
5. How do you continue to envision your future without your parents?

CONTRIBUTORS

Rosanna Arquette currently stars in the television series *What About Brian*. Arquette has appeared in more than seventy films, including *Pulp Fiction* and *Desperately Seeking Susan*. She has also directed and produced two highly acclaimed documentaries, *Searching for Debra Winger* and *All We Are Saying*. Her mother died of cancer when Arquette was thirty-eight; her father died of complications from a liver transplant when she was forty-one.

Yogi Berra is a National Baseball Hall of Fame legend. Berra is a fifteen-time All-Star and has won more world championships than any other baseball player in history. In all, he played in fourteen World Series. Berra's mother died of diabetes when he was thirty-four; he was thirty-six when his father passed away from heart trouble.

Dana Buchman is a fashion designer. Buchman's line of clothing is one of the most broadly distributed designer labels for women in the country. She is also the author of *A Special Education*—the story of her daughter Charlotte's lifelong struggle with severe learning disabilities. Buchman's father died of a stroke when she was thirty; she was forty-three when her mother died of a heart attack.

ROSANNE CASH is a Grammy-award-winning singer and song-writer. Cash has recorded nearly a dozen albums, including her most recent smash hit, *Black Cadillac*. Her other records include *Interiors, The Wheel,* and *10 Song Demo*. Her father, music legend Johnny Cash, died from complications of diabetes when she was forty-eight; she was fifty when her mother died from an infection following surgery for lung cancer.

CARMELA CIURARU is a writer, editor, and author of seven poetry anthologies, including *First Loves: Poets Introduce the Essential Poems That Captivated and Inspired Them* and *Solitude: Poems*. Ciuraru is a regular contributor to the *Los Angeles Times, More, Spin,* and other publications and is currently working on a nonfiction book. Her mother battled breast cancer, but died suddenly of an aneurysm when Ciuraru was sixteen; her father died of colon cancer when she was twenty-one.

TERRANCE DEAN is the founder of Men's Empowerment, Inc., a not-for-profit organization dedicated to empowering the lives of men of color. Dean is also the author of the best-selling book *Reclaim Your Power!: A 30-Day Guide to Hope, Healing, and Inspiration for*

Men of Color. Dean's father was shot to death when he was twelve; his mother died of AIDS when he was twenty-one.

HOPE EDELMAN is the author of *The New York Times* bestseller *Motherless Daughters* and its sister title, *Letters from Motherless Daughters.* Edelman's latest book is called *Motherless Mothers.* Besides being a writer, she also lectures extensively on this subject. Edelman's mother died from breast cancer when she was seventeen; her father passed away, also from cancer, when she was forty.

BARBARA EHRENREICH is the author of thirteen books, including *The New York Times* bestseller *Nickel and Dimed.* A contributing writer for *Time* magazine, she also writes frequently for *The New York Times, Harper's,* and *The Progressive.* Ehrenreich was thirty-five when her mother died from a likely suicide; her father died years later from Alzheimer's disease.

GERALDINE FERRARO is the first woman selected as a vice presidential candidate on a national party ticket. Ferraro has also been a member of the U.S. House of Representatives—serving New York's 9th Congressional District in Queens for three terms. She is currently a senior managing director and chair of the Public Affairs practice of the Global Consulting Group. Ferraro's father died of a heart attack when she was eight; she was fifty-four when her mother died of emphysema.

DENNIS FRANZ is an actor best known for his four-time Emmy-award-winning role as Detective Andy Sipowicz on the hit television show *NYPD Blue*. He also had a recurring role in the TV series *Hill Street Blues*. Franz has appeared in numerous films, including *City of Angels* and *Die Hard 2: Die Harder*. At the age of forty, Franz lost his father to cancer and his mother just months later to a stroke.

KATE CARLSON FURER is the owner of Physicians Weight Loss Center in Plantation, Florida. Prior to opening this business, Furer worked in sales and purchasing in the Garment District in New York City. She was twenty-nine when she lost her mom to cancer; her father suffered from Parkinson's disease and died in his sleep when Furer was thirty.

JEFF GELMAN is a freelance journalist. Gelman's work has been published in various newspapers, including the *Philadelphia City Paper, The Morning Call,* and the *Delaware County Daily Times.* During his ten-year career as a newspaper reporter, he has won numerous awards. Gelman's parents were killed by a drunk driver when he was fourteen.

MARIEL HEMINGWAY is an actress and author and the granddaughter of Ernest Hemingway. Hemingway made her silver-screen debut in the movie *Lipstick,* and her work in Woody Allen's *Manhattan* earned her an Oscar nomination. Her books include *Finding My Balance* and the forthcoming *Living in Balance*. Hemingway was twenty-eight when her mother died of lung disease; her father died from complications following heart bypass surgery when she was thirty-nine.

ICE-T is an actor and Grammy-award-winning singer currently starring as Detective Fin on *Law & Order: Special Victims Unit*. Ice-T is credited with inventing gangsta rap and was an honoree in VH1's 2005 *Hip Hop Honors*. He is also a sought-after public speaker—lecturing on college campuses across the country about the dangers facing young adults today. Ice-T's mother died of a heart attack when he was seven; his father also succumbed to a heart attack when he was eleven.

SHELBY LYNNE is a country and R&B singer who won a Grammy award for Best New Artist in 2001. Her latest album, *Suit Yourself*, was released to critical acclaim. Her prior albums include *Identity Crisis; Love, Shelby;* and *I Am Shelby Lynne*. She was seventeen when her father fatally shot her mother before turning the gun on himself.

CATHERYNE ILKOVIC MORGAN is a Holocaust survivor. Morgan's parents were both killed in Auschwitz, the infamous concentration camp, when she was fourteen. She has been a volunteer for more than ten years at the Evelyn H. Lauder Breast Center, a division of the Memorial Sloan-Kettering Cancer Center, and was recently awarded the Volunteer of the Year medal.

BRIAN O'HARA is a sales assistant at ABC television network. O'Hara was twelve when both of his parents and his sister were killed aboard TWA flight 800. The Paris-bound flight crashed in the waters off Long Island, New York on July 17, 1996. O'Hara graduated from Boston College in 2005.

PAMELA REDMOND SATRAN is the author of four novels— *Suburbanistas, Younger, Babes in Captivity,* and *The Man I Should Have Married*—and the coauthor of several best-selling baby-naming guides, including *Beyond Jennifer & Jason.* Satran is a contributing editor for *Parenting* and a columnist for *Glamour;* her articles and essays have appeared in numerous publications, including *The New York Times, More,* and *Redbook.* Her mother died when Satran was thirty from complications related to a lifetime of severe rheumatoid arthritis; her father passed away due to emphysema when she was thirty-eight.

SERGEANT MICHAEL TREANOR is assigned to the Plans and Operations unit of the 45th Infantry Brigade, Oklahoma Army National Guard. Sergeant Treanor has been in the military, in various divisions, since 1980. His parents were both killed in the bombing of the Alfred P. Murrah Federal Building in Oklahoma City on April 19, 1995, when he was thirty-one.

VALERIE WEBB is a senior in high school. Her mother died of a heart attack when she was ten; her father, a Port Authority police officer, was killed one year later when he responded to the September 11 terrorist attacks at the World Trade Center in New York City.

ACKNOWLEDGMENTS

IN MY HOME OFFICE, I have a plastic binder full of letters that I hope will one day provide an invaluable life lesson for my children. The notes are not words of praise for my work as a writer and award-winning television news producer. They are not correspondence related to any of the talented and important people I have interviewed over the years. They are the rejection letters, sorted chronologically and kept in pristine condition, that I received from publishers big and small across the country related to this book. There was never going to be a threshold of negative letters that would make me walk away from this project; I was like a pit bull. Having lost both my parents, I knew this book would help other people who were in the same situation. I kept searching for a publisher that would understand why it needed to be published. My husband was concerned I would get a concussion from banging my head against the wall.

Then Jill Rothenberg, a wonderful editor at Seal Press, showed the interest I had been hoping for. From our first conversation, she was on board and in my corner. Jill, your support made my dream come true. A special word of thanks goes to the string of women who put me in touch with Jill in the first place: Eileen McCaffrey of the Orphan Foundation of America put me in touch with Martha Shirk. It was ultimately Martha who suggested I call Jill. Martha, that advice was life-changing.

This book would not have been possible without the courageous participation of the people who agreed to be interviewed. Their honesty and willingness to bare so much of themselves will no doubt help countless others. I thank each of them for trusting me with their most intimate thoughts and memories. I am grateful to them beyond measure.

I also owe many thanks to the agents, publicists, personal managers, and supportive contacts and friends who graciously helped get interview requests to many of the contributors in this book. They are: LaDonna Battle, Dale Berra, Jeff Blagg, Lauren Cuneo, Karyn Curtis, Maria Darch, Adam Griffin, Andrea Herbert, Alan Hicks, Jorge Hinojosa, Elizabeth Jordan, Danny Kahn, Judi Kerr, Barbara Mahon, Joy and Paul Mandel, Lucy Milby, Joyce Miltz, Lani Mustacchi, Peggy O'Hara, Edith Petway, Leo Rechter, Jenny Rosenstrach, Cynthia Snyder, Jane Thomas, Kari Watkins, and Lea Yardum.

Gratitude goes to my agent, Angela Miller, and my wonderful editor, Christina Baker Kline. Christina, I feel lucky to have worked with you on this project and I'm even more fortunate to call you my friend.

A thank-you also to Chris Kirkpatrick of Transcript Associates for ensuring that dozens of hours of audiotape were transcribed with speed and accuracy. And a warm thank-you to Douglas Smith, who runs Korakia, a hotel in Palm Springs, California. The hotel was the perfect venue for my interview with Shelby Lynne.

Particular appreciation goes to my family and friends, who for years endured countless (I am sure they'd say "tedious") conversations about "the book." I thank you for being in my corner and never telling me to pack it in.

And to my husband and best friend, Mark—where do I begin to thank you? You never complained when I asked you to read, and then reread, these chapters. Your enthusiastic input made this book better. You make me laugh, cry . . . incredibly happy. I am lucky to have you in my life.

To my two children, Jake and Lexi, who had to put up with Mommy being busy in her office "again." I love you.

As for that binder in my office, I will take it out whenever my children doubt their ability to get something done or pursue their dreams. This book is proof that if you believe in something with enough passion and commitment, you can make it happen.

ABOUT THE AUTHOR

ALLISON GILBERT is a producer for CNN's *American Morning*. A three-time Emmy award-winning investigative journalist, she has produced special projects for WABC-TV in New York, worked as an investigative producer for WNBC-TV, and helped launch MSNBC as a writer and special assignments producer. She has written numerous articles for newspapers and magazines, and she coedited the book *Covering Catastrophe: Broadcast Journalists Report September 11*. She lives in New York with her husband, Mark, and their two children. Visit Allison at **www.alwaystoosoon.com**.

ABOUT THE EDITOR

CHRISTINA BAKER KLINE is a novelist, nonfiction writer, and freelance editor. Her new novel, *The Way Life Should Be*, will come out in 2007. You can visit Christina at **www.christinabakerkline.com**.

SELECTED TITLES
from Seal Press

For more than thirty years, Seal Press has published groundbreaking books. By women. For women. Visit our website at **www.sealpress.com**.

Another Morning: Voices of Truth and Hope From Mothers With Cancer by Linda Blachman. $15.95, 1-58005-178-2. A collection of powerful, inspirational, and deeply moving personal stories of ordinary women responding to every mother's nightmare: a cancer diagnosis while raising children.

Above Us Only Sky: A Woman Looks Back, Ahead, and into the Mirror by Marion Winik. $14.95, 1-58005-144-8. A witty and engaging book from NPR commentator Marion Winik about facing midlife without getting tangled up in the past or hung up in the future.

Planet Widow: A Mother's Story of Navigating a Suddenly Unrecognizable World by Gloria Lenhart. $14.95, 1-58005-168-5. This book chronicles the events after the unexpected death of a spouse, and offers support for other widows.

Literary Mama: Reading for the Maternally Inclined edited by Andrea J. Buchanan and Amy Hudock. $14.95, 1-58005-158-8. From the best of literarymama.com, this collection of personal writing includes creative nonfiction, fiction, and poetry.

Solo: On Her Own Adventure edited by Susan Fox Rogers. $15.95, 1-58005-137-5. An inspiring collection of travel narratives that reveal the complexities of women journeying alone.

I Wanna Be Sedated: 30 Writers on Parenting Teenagers edited by Faith Conlon and Gail Hudson. $15.95, 1-58005-127-8. With hilarious and heartfelt essays, this anthology will reassure any parent of a teenager that they are not alone in their desire to be comatose.